Organizational Proctology

Field Notes for Dealing with Asshats in the Workplace

Pete Hammett

DEDICATION

This book is dedicated to those individuals who've encountered difficult people in the workplace and suffered from asshole-related-stress (ARSe). My sincerest hope and fervent prayer are that this book provides the insight and advice that allows ARSe sufferers to recover, heal and move forward.

Table of Contents

ACKNOWLEDGMENTS

This book is the culmination of years of experience helping those who've suffered deeply from their encounters with workplace assholes, years of experience coaching assholes to consider the terrible legacy they create, and years of experience advising organizations how they can create a culture that invests in their most valuable resource—their people. During this journey I've had the great honor to partner with countless business leaders, behavioral scientists, psychiatrists, psychologists, medical doctors and organizational development consultants.

I could write an entire chapter acknowledging those who have provided me guidance and encouragement as this book came together. Doing so, though, would come with a cost. The unfortunate reality of dealing with assholes in the workplace is the hatefulness that embodies the very worst of them. Throughout this book I reference real-life stories of people behaving badly in the workplace. In each case I've been mindful to change the names of specific people and details of organizations to provide a level of anonymity to those who might otherwise become the target of asshole vindictiveness.

With this in mind: To my wonderful friends and colleagues whose insights, counsel and thought partnership were incalculable in creating this body of work, I extend my deepest gratitude.

About the Author

Dr. Pete Hammett has over 25 years in talent management ranging from organization culture, to employee engagement, to leadership development, to coaching. Pete speaks regularly at business and human resources conferences and is a guest lecturer at Purdue University.

Prior to starting Hammett Consulting, Pete was the head of human resources and talent Management at OGE Energy Corporation—a regulated electric utility whose 2,400 employees serve more than 800,000 customers in Oklahoma and Arkansas. In 2011 Pete won the Chief Learning Officer of the Year award.

Pete held the position of director of client services and senior faculty at the Center for Creative Leadership (CCL), the world's foremost provider of executive education. For more than four decades CCL has aligned the science and practice of leadership to transform individuals, teams and organizations to achieve results that are powerful, measurable and enduring. While at CCL Pete published **Unbalanced Influence,** a book that expounds the paradoxes and expels the myths of executive leadership. Pete also won the 2009 Outstanding Paper from Emerald Literati Networks (Europe) for "The Paradox of Gifted Leadership: Developing the Next Generation of Leaders."

Pete's business experience encompasses several key positions at American Express, including vice president for operations and technology, where he was in charge of relationship management and business process optimization. While at Amex, Pete also served as director of new product development and was responsible for building the business and relationship management framework for Amex's co-branding and affinity products.

Pete had a distinguished career in aerospace and defense (ILC Dover) where he designed the technical platform for allocating spacesuits to Shuttle flight crews.

Pete holds a doctorate of strategic leadership from Regent University, an MBA from Wilmington University, and a BS in computer science from Wesley University.

Chapter 1: First Things First

WHY I WROTE THIS BOOK

There's an epidemic emerging that the Centers for Disease Control and Prevention (CDC) hasn't yet catalogued. The physical symptomatology is very concerning: chronic headaches, muscle tension, fatigue, and issues regulating both sleep and eating. The psychological impacts are equally alarming: reduced aspiration, diminished sense of confidence, and emotional detachment.

To help the CDC identify this condition I've named the epidemic asshole-related-stress (ARSe, pronounced just like its spelled). ARSe is the condition that emerges in the workplace when a person sees no way out of miserable interactions with a terrible boss or a jerk co-worker.

Asshole-related-stress (ARSe) is the condition that emerges in the workplace when a person sees no way out of miserable interactions with a terrible boss or a jerk co-worker.

My first encounter with ARSe occurred many years ago when my daughter, Nancy called and spoke six heartbreaking words… "*Daddy, I really need your help*". I can still hear the conversation in my mind all these years later. A year earlier, Nancy finished college and landed her first job with a national marketing firm. She was doing great, earning a few advancements within her first 12 months. Her contributions were being noticed by others and she was approached by another department manager about an opening in their area. But when Nancy spoke to her boss, Jane, about the opportunity, things went south in a major way. Jane became verbally abusive, accusing Nancy of being disloyal and unappreciative. Jane began to run down and belittle Nancy's work over the past year. Then Jane made it clear that she would see to it that no one would want Nancy in their department. Since Nancy's initial conversation with Jane, things at the office had become absolutely miserable. Jane was constantly berating Nancy's work and she was piling on some of the most menial tasks. Nancy's colleagues sought to console her, telling stories of how Jane had similarly treated them.

During this time, I held an executive position with the Center for Creative Leadership (CCL). CCL is one of foremost organizations in the world dedicated to leadership development and executive coaching. In this role I was afforded the privilege of working with some of the best minds in the field of leadership research. I also had the unique opportunity to work alongside some remarkable global leaders. My daughter Nancy, of course, knew all this and her tearful voice cracked over the phone: "Dad, you help other leaders do better. Can't you come here and help us?"

Damn. How do you answer that? I tried explaining to my daughter that it just doesn't work that way. Leaders need to want to lead better; they can't be forced to be better leaders. We talked for a long time. I offered some generic career advice, which made me feel useful but frankly didn't help Nancy much. The hard fact is this: There is no external "fix" for someone who is hell-bent on being a jerk. We can draw on psychology and neuroscience to better understand why people behave in an asinine manner. But the "fix" for bad behavior has to come from within. Nancy stayed with the firm another 6 months. Things didn't improve, and she left for a much better firm and a really great boss.

Unfortunately, Nancy's story is not isolated. To the contrary, the volume of hard science and anecdotal evidence points clearly to two undeniable conclusions: (1) There are too many assholes in the workplace and (2) the madness these people create has to stop. That's why I wrote this book!

ORGANIZATIONAL PROCTOLOGY

Organizational proctology[1] is the study of assholes in the workplace, along with the treatment and prevention of (ARSe). To be clear, there are awful people all over the place. We could just as easily talk about educational proctology or congregational proctology (yes there are abrasive people in church—but most recognize their failings and are recovering). We might even consider governmental proctology, but what would be the point? For the purpose of this book we'll keep our focus on a-holes in the workplace.

FIELD NOTES

Field notes is a method of journaling: a systematic approach to keeping a log of the various experiences you encounter. Those trained in behavioral sciences such as psychology, cultural anthropology, and sociology refine their skills of observation so they can readily capture and recall key insights about the behaviors, activities, emotions and outcomes associated with the events being observed. For the novice (folks like me), the art and practice of keeping field notes provides some helpful disciplines:

(1) When organized and studied, field notes help produce meaning and understanding of the culture, social situation or human interaction being studied.
(2) By the very nature of capturing field notes, you not only interact with those you are observing, you are also prompted to define your relationship with those you study. Thus affecting how you choose to see the world being

---

[1] I want to apologize to those medical professionals who are proctologists. Since turning a certain age, I have a new found appreciation for your work. Please know I mean no disrespect to your profession in co-opting the term proctology. Over the years, as I've developed this book, the term organizational proctology has emerged as a meaningful expression that connects with ARSe suffers in a very powerful way.

observed. In other words, you are both *recording the story* and are *part of the story* at the same time.[2]

For the past several years, I've undertaken the keeping, organizing, and reflecting on countless interactions with workplace assholes. Some of these interactions are from my own personal experiences dealing with them; however many (too many) come from counseling those dealing with them. I also draw on interactions in which I directly coach terrible leaders—some who turned over a new leaf and others who turned a blind eye. These field notes serve as the basis for this book.

SORRY, MOM!

If books carried ratings like movies, this one might be a PG-13 type of book—solely based on the use of one very provocative word: *asshole*. I understand that for some people using this term will be offensive, and may cause them to avoid this book altogether.
Case in Point:

Here's how the conversation unfolded when I called my father to run the idea of this book by him:

Me: "Hey, Dad I have an idea for my next book. I'm calling it *Organizational Proctology: Field Notes for Dealing with Assholes in the Workplace*. What do you think?"

Dad: (laughing) "I don't think your mother is going to like 'asshole' in the title."

Mom: (in the background) "Watch your language!"

Dad: "Told you!"

---

[2] I recall seeing a story of a well-known newscaster reporting on Vietnamese boat people. The reporter was on shore giving his update while in the background several flimsy boats overflowing with refugees, struggled to reach the shore. While on camera one of the boats capsized about 100 yards from shore—and women and small children were thrown in the water. The reporter jumped into the water and began rescuing people. After the event some criticized the reporter, saying you can't "report on" the story and "be the story" at the same time. I really don't recall exactly how the reporter responded. But in my mind I heard them say "bull."

For each person who is offended by this phrase, however, there are an equal or greater number that will have the opposite reaction— finding the term 100% appropriate and quickly resonating with the subject matter. My interest, though, in using the term is not as a gimmick to grab attention or provoke disapproval.

As I began thinking about writing this book, I did what many authors do: a bit of field testing. Each year I have the honor of speaking with various business, government, and academic organizations across the U.S. While organizational proctology has seldom been the headline topic, I often float the concept in my presentations as well as in offline conversations. I can say that, without exception, each time I begin a conversation with folks about dealing with "asshats" in the workplace, I hear a strong affirmation from the group. So much so that within a short time, others are sharing their war stories of dealing with such people. So after spending a considerable amount of time pondering if and how I might apply the term, I've locked in on using *asshole* to identify those people whose behavior really, really sets us off.

A BRIEF HISTORY OF THE TERM

Let's be frank. The term *asshole* is commonly used as a vulgar insult. For kids its use is often followed by a thorough washing out of their mouth with soap. Strictly speaking, when used as slang to describe a person's actions the term typically describes one of two behaviors: (a) that which is stupid and mindless or (b) behavior that is mean and contemptible. How did the word *asshole* evolve? Who was the first to use the word? Who was the first person to be called an *asshole*? What is the history of the term?

According to Geoffery Nunberg the use of *asshole* may have emerged as a "personal description in the 'barracks slang' of World War II, and ever since then it has been a label for an arrogant or overbearing superior." Nunberg goes on to describe how it came into literary and then contemporary parlance by way of authors such as Neil

Simon, Woody Allen, Tom Wolfe, and, most notably, Norman Mailer (in his1948 work *The Naked and the Dead*). While the outright use of the *asshole* can offend those with more delicate sensibilities, our vocabulary is quite at peace with the concept—as evidenced by the widely accepted adjective *asinine* in describing foolish or silly behavior.

To be honest, you can easily use other words—such as jerk, and knucklehead. Few phrases, however, bring greater passion and emotion to the conversation. When we are describing a person's behavior, particularly in the workplace, the term is much more than a swear word. *Asshole* quickly resonates with people. When you're sharing with someone that a boss or co-worker is an *asshole* you seldom need to say anything more.

It's as if there's a universal link among all humankind that allows us in one instant to come together in a perfect harmony. Let's be completely honest; there is a bit of catharsis when we use the term. Without needing to explain or embellish any further, we can simply say, *"They're an absolute asshole,"* and in one moment it feels both complete and cleansing.

Consider our reaction when someone cuts us off in traffic. Why is our first response to shout, "Asshole!"—even if no one is in the car with you. (Come-on, you know you do it.) According to Aaron James, the reason we shout this is to reassure ourselves, and those with us, that we clearly understand and recognize common civil behavior; and we're not afraid to point out when the line between civility and anarchy has been crossed: all from the safety of our car, ever mindful not to incite road rage. So, too, when we goof up and make a mess of things—be it spill a drink, stub a toe or really foul up a relationship. Psychologist Steven Pinker observes how when we call out our own missteps with words like oops, goober, and nuts, we are informing those around us that we know we made a mistake, that we didn't intentionally drop a slice of pizza in our lap. And on the rare occasion when we really foul things up, such as saying or doing the worst thing at the worst time, we will call ourselves out as an a-hole.

ASSHAT VS. "ASSHOLE"

Now that I've apologized to my mom and explained why I've chosen to use the term "asshole", I need to let readers know that in this book I'll often switch between the terms Asshat, Asshole, A-hole, jerk, etc. The reason is simply pragmatic. A few years back I had the rare honor of speaking to a large group of Chief-Human-Resource Officers on "Organizational Proctology: Field notes for dealing with assholes in the workplace." What I learned from this experience is that nearly half of the invitations where blocked by company email filters because I used *asshole* in the title of the program. The second thing I learned was word-of-mouth readily overcomes company email filters. Still, it seems pragmatic to measure the use of the "A-word."

I'M SURROUNDED BY ASSHOLES

At times it seems like everywhere we go we run into assholes. When we go out to dinner it's not uncommon to find a customer or waiter behaving badly. If you are flying and there's an unexpected delay, the asshats seem to come out in force. As noted earlier, it's almost a certainty you'll encounter at least one a-hole when you're driving. Without question, a-holes abound at work (sometimes it seems like companies go out of their way to either hire or grow asshat employees). It can be so overwhelming at times that you might be tempted to misquote the poem "The Charge of the Light Brigade":

> Assholes to the right of me,
> Assholes to the left of me,
> Assholes in front of me;
> Volley'd and thunder'd;
> Storm'd at with shot and shell,
> Boldly I rode and well,
> into the jaws of a toxic workplace.

DEFINING ASININE BEHAVIOR

Right from the start let's make a very important distinction between a person's behavior and their character. More to the point, when we describe a person's behavior, we are not in the same breath judging their character. Many of us will recall the admonishment, "Don't call someone stupid." This is as true today as when we heard it as kids. Calling someone stupid is wrong, period. While subtle, there is a difference between describing a person's actions as "mindless" and calling them stupid.

The same is true for describing our own emotions. We often will say, "I'm depressed" when what we truly are saying is, "I feel depressed." So when we say someone is an asshole, what we're doing is characterizing their behavior. It's just easier to say "They're an a-hole" than, "They're behaving like a jerk." That said, how do we define asinine behavior?

I'm not talking about those folks who have a quirky mannerism or occasionally say or do something that's annoying. Nor am I referring to those of us who at one time or another had a mental meltdown and acted like a complete jerk. I'm talking about those people who are a constant pain, who just seem to be bent on behaving in a way that is self-centered, spiteful, and vindictive.

Later in this book I'll expand the definition of a workplace asshole in detail, but for now let's start with this: Such a person is someone whose persistent pattern of behavior can be described with one or more of these characteristics:

- Manipulative, deceitful, callous, mean-spirited, arrogant
- Self-Centered (overly concerned for how they are seen / perceived)
- Self-Absorbed (high view of themselves that they regularly express and look for others to validate publicly)
- Regularly takes advantage of others (quick to use others as cannon fodder to advance their own self-interests)
- Difficultly relating with the feelings of others

THE GOLDWATER RULE

During and after the 2016 election and the less-than-presidential behavior of President Trump, a debate has resurfaced within the behavioral science community:

'Is it ethical for a mental health professional to define or label the actions of a public figure, or to take this to the extreme, make assertions regarding a public figure's fitness to hold office?'

At the heart of this debate are the American Psychiatric Association[3] ethical guidelines "for responsibly participating in activities that contribute to the improvement of the community and the betterment of public health." Specifically, the guideline reads as follows:

On occasion psychiatrists are asked for an opinion about an individual who is in the light of public attention or who has disclosed information about himself/herself through public media. In such circumstances, a psychiatrist may share with the public his or her expertise about psychiatric issues in general. However, it is unethical for a psychiatrist to offer a professional opinion unless he or she has conducted an examination and has been granted proper authorization for such a statement (Section 7, number 3, in *The Principles of Medical Ethics with Annotations Especially Applicable to Psychiatry*, 2013 edition).

---

[3] If the field of behavioral science wasn't complicated enough, we have the added confusion of distinguishing between two communities of practice: the American Psychological Association and the American Psychiatric Association—both of whom use APA as their call sign. (Neither of which should be confused with the American Pool-players Association, who also use the call sign APA.) A 2010 Time article does a good job summarizing the feud between the Psychological and Psychiatric associations. [http://healthland.time.com/2010/10/01/psychology-vs-psychiatry-whats-the-difference-and-which-is-better/]; and the Psychological Association does a fine job explaining the educational differences between psychologists and psychologists [https://www.apa.org/ptsd-guideline/patients-and-families/psychotherapy-professionals.pdf].

This guideline, known as the Goldwater Rule, came into play as a result of the 1964 presidential race between President Lyndon B. Johnson and Barry Goldwater, Republican senator from Arizona. During the campaign Goldwater was harshly criticized by over 1,000 psychiatrists as being "unpredictable," "emotionally unstable," "a dangerous lunatic," "paranoid," "counterfeit figure of a masculine man," and having a "Godlike self-image." The consensus from these mental health professionals was that Goldwater was unfit to be president. Goldwater lost the election, but won the subsequent lawsuit for libel. The Goldwater Rule, established in 1973, is an attempt by the APA to say, "You can't diagnose a mental disorder unless you've examined the patient." And you can't speak publicly about a patient's condition without their permission.

The Goldwater Rule is under significant scrutiny with nearly every tweet from President Trump. Those who would disregard the rule suggest it is in the public's best interest for professionals in mental health care to take part in the discussion about Trump's behavior. Some argue that the Goldwater Rule is a medical ethics standard and that it only applies to psychiatrists and not to psychologists or psychoanalysts. One thing is clear, the debate over the Goldwater rule will continue for some time.

For me, the whole thing sounds like the argument about whether Pluto is a planet. If it looks like a plant and it acts like a planet, then it's a planet. For the most part, in this book, I will address the behaviors that are attributable to asshats. Like most people I can identify with great certainty and without clinical diagnosis, the assholes I've encountered in the workplace.

CULTURAL VIEW OF ASSHOLES

If it is true that art imitates life, then we have ample proof in the multitude of asshats depicted in movies. I must say that the depth of subject matter goes well beyond the typical antagonist needed for a movie to work. Consider this: A Google search on "assholes in the movies" returns over 18 million hits: 18 million! That's a lot. Here are a few notables many of us will remember:

Principle Rooney in *Ferris Bueller's Day Off*
Shooter McGavin in *Happy Gilmore*
Richard "Dick" Vernon in *The Breakfast Club*
Biff in *Back to the Future*
Bill Lumbergh in *Office Space*
Buddy Ackerman in *Swimming with Sharks*
Three characters in *Horrible Bosses*

The term asshole has not only become a common place descriptor of poor behavior; we can even use it to define and measure our social condition. For example:

Assholism **Assholery** [Tomfoolery]	**Asshole-a-tude** **Anti-Asshole** [State of being (or not being) an asshole]	**Assholization** [Progression towards a higher level of asshole behavior]

STORY OF AN ASSHAT—SMALL MAN/BIG EGO

Throughout this book I'll share stories of workplace ass-clowns. While these are real stories, I've changed the names and some details just a bit to keep the story accurate and specific people and companies discreet.

As you read these stories, you'll most likely see common threads from your own experiences. I share these stories to help those suffering from ARSe connect with others who have similar experiences. I also share these stories to help recovering a-holes recognize their own behaviors—and hopefully ask themselves, "Is this really how I behave, and do I want to be seen this way?"

Here's my first story. When two nationally recognized banks headquartered in New York City merged, the new board of directors were faced with a dilemma: who to name as the CEO of the new firm. While either CEO from the two original banks could have stepped into the leadership role, the board didn't want to give the impression that one bank held a stronger position than its counterpart. So the board decided to find a CEO from the outside. After a lengthy nationwide search, Frank was hired to take the CEO role.

Before his first day on the job rumors surfaced that he had a reputation for being a really poor leader: someone who micro-managed his direct reports and often became distracted with lower level operational details. Within the first few weeks of joining the company the rumors proved understated. Frank was much, much worse.

While his physical stature was below average, his ego was larger than life. Everything and everybody were expected to revolve around him. First he sought to move the company's headquarters and its hundreds of corporate employees to Charlotte—so he and his family wouldn't have to move. When the board denied this request, Frank refused to move to New York City and instead took out a multiyear lease on an executive apartment there, the cost of which he demanded the bank cover. Then Frank required his direct reports to change their work schedules to accommodate his flying into the city late Monday morning and leaving Friday afternoon.

Day to day, Frank was rude, obnoxious, and condescending. No one dared to disagree or challenge him. If they did, there was hell to pay. Within the first 2 months of joining the bank Frank initiated a significant reorganization—only to be revised twice within a 4 week period.

And the stories about him grew each day. There was the story where he refused to interview an executive assistant because she didn't wear a dress to the interview. And countless stories of 2 a.m. e-mails that Frank expected to be answered before 8 a.m. that day (including weekends). The best story about Frank was how proud he was that the board felt he was the only and best leader for the bank among the bank's existing leadership team, which in Frank's mind gave him a mandate to do as he pleased and ignore input from others.

Within 4 months the rancor within the executive team stemming from Frank's ego-centric behavior became too much. Over the next few months several executives defected, often with major clients following. Eventually, the board's concern for the viability of the bank under Frank's leadership was such that he was asked to leave (with an unbelievable severance package).

WHERE DO WE GO FROM HERE?

Our experience tells us the world is full of difficult people. But why is that? What's going on in someone's head that makes them think it's okay or a good idea to be an asshole? And how do we definitively define asinine behavior. Is there a "scale" we can use to measure the degree of asinine behavior? Is there is a difference between being a jerk and being an asshole? Most importantly, how can you deal with the asshat in your workplace? Is your only option to leave or should you just tolerate a terrible situation? The remainder of this book will take you on a journey to answer these questions.

The first part—chapters 2 through 5——will help you understand why people act badly at work, and the second part—chapters 6 through 10—will provide you with a framework for dealing with such behavior and its effect on you. Finally, because not all bad behavior is conscious or intentional, the appendix will help you reflect on whether you yourself are acting like an asshole and, if so, how (whether) you can change.

Chapter 2: The Science of Asshole Behavior

In 2001 psychiatrists Thomas Lewis, Fari Amini and Richard Lannon wrote a book entitled *The General Theory of Love*. Below is an excerpt from a New York Times review in which the authors describe their work:

What is love, and why are some people unable to find it? What is loneliness, and why does it hurt? What are relationships, and how and why do they work the way they do?

Answering these questions, laying bare the heart's deepest secrets, is this book's aim. Since the dawn of our species, human beings in every time and place have contended with an unruly emotional core that behaves in unpredicted and confusing ways. Science has been unable to help them. The Western world's first physician, Hippocrates, proposed in 450 B.C. that emotions emanate from the brain. He was right—but for the next twenty-five hundred years, medicine could offer nothing further about the details of emotional life. Matters of the heart were matters only for the arts—literature, song, poetry, painting, sculpture, and dance.

The past decade has seen an explosion of scientific discoveries about the brain, the leading edge of a revolution that promises to change the way we think about ourselves, our relationships, our children, and our society. Science can at last turn its penetrating gaze on humanity's oldest questions. Its revelations stand poised to shatter more than a few modern assumptions about the inner workings of love...

Lewis, Amini and Lannon's book helped advance our understanding of the why, who and how we love. In the spirit of Lewis and his colleagues, I'll frame a general theory of assholes and outline the psychology and neuroscience behind why people behave that way. But first let's look at a couple of important issues.

THE DIFFERENCE BETWEEN "ACTING LIKE" AND "BEING" AN ASSHAT

Everyone acts like an asshat at some point. It's inevitable. Someone or something will push just the right button and you'll lose your cool[4]. But just because you lose it occasionally and act really badly, does that make you an asshat? Our initial instinct would be to say "No." An occasional slip into poor behavior shouldn't define me as an asshat. The real question then is what distinguishes the person who occasionally exhibits asinine behavior from the dyed-in-the-wool asshat? The answer centers on a person's underlying beliefs (how they view the world) and how these beliefs influence how they behave.

Assholes are those who exhibit a predictable pattern of callous manipulative, arrogant and self-absorbed behavior from which a toxic and harmful workplace environment emerges.

We can extend a measure of grace to someone who loses their temper and acts foolishly; we've all done this. However, the behavior of an asshole in the workplace is far from occasional. They exhibit a predictable pattern of callous, manipulative, arrogant, and self-absorbed behavior from which a toxic and harmful workplace environment emerges.

THE LUCIFER EFFECT

Philip Zimbardo may be best known for the creation and execution of the Stanford Prison Experiment. In 1971 Zimbardo, a psychology professor at Stanford, received funding from the U.S. Navy to investigate the psychological effects between prison guards and prisoners—specifically how the power associated with guards influenced and impacted the interaction with prisoners. He designed the experiment using Stanford students to play the role of prison guards and prisoners, with him playing the role of prison superintendent. After only a few days the students became lost in their

---

[4] Check out "brain jacking" in Chapter 7 ("Dealing with Workplace Assholes").

roles (as did Zimbardo). Guards began to exert their power over prisoners in disturbing and brutal fashion.

At first the guards' behavior was subtle—for instance, choosing to refer to prisoners by their number, not their name. However, within days prisoners were punished with extended exercise and forced to endure unsanitary conditions; they were made to sleep on concrete floors and forced to be naked. The psychological and emotional impacts caused by the mistreatment of students playing the role of prisoners was so bad that the experiment was halted after 6 days.

As you might expect, the Stanford Prison Experiment has received both interest and criticism. Still, the observations from the experiment provided Zimbardo with first hand insights into how "good" people can do "bad" things. To this end, he became an expert witness in the Abu Ghraib investigation.

In 2008 Zimbardo wrote *The Lucifer Effect,* which detailed the events and outcomes from the Stanford Prison Experiment. In this book, Zimbardo sets forth a fascinating description of evil when he writes: "Evil consists in intentionally behaving in ways that harm, abuse, demean, dehumanize, or destroy innocent others—or using one's authority and systemic power to encourage or permit others to do so on your behalf."

In the appendix (Are You an Asshole?) I'll define the varying degrees of bad behavior: from "Level 1—Annoying Prick" (those who are so miserable with the world and their place in it that they make it their goal to create misery for others), to "Level 5—Flaming Asshole" (those who seem to feed off the anxiety and stress they create).

GENERAL THEORY OF ASSHOLES

To help us understand why people behave like an asshole, it's helpful to define an overarching general theory of assholes:

- Assholes emerge principally from an overwhelming conviction that they are immeasurably gifted beyond most people and therefore due success, status, and, most of all, privilege—chief of which is the right to use and exploit others in order to advance their own agenda/purpose.

- Asinine behavior stems first and foremost from selfish and self-centered motivations—which in turn are fueled by a deep-seated, paranoid mistrust as they expect the worst in others. This is why assholes regularly confuse loyalty with integrity.

- Asshat behavior can likewise emerge from a delusional sense of "greater good" or "higher purpose." So if some people are used as cannon fodder for the good of the cause, or if certain rules of social convention are ignored, or if infractions are made against legal or moral code, then so be it—as long as their view of the greater good is achieved.

- Finally, not only are assholes comfortable manipulating and misusing others for personal advancement, they also gain an aberrant sense of satisfaction in creating misery for others. Assholes are acutely aware of the disruption, anxiety, and turmoil they create, and they enjoy it.

The genesis that spawns nearly every asshat is a recognized giftedness in a sought-after skill or character trait: an engineer that is brilliant in solving the toughest problems; a lawyer that is masterful in litigating high-profile cases; a business executive that is charismatic and personable; a physician well known for their medical skills. Over time the person racks up one success after the other, along with mounting accolades, promotions, and bonuses. The perceived value to the organization or society from the

> **The genesis that spawns nearly every asshat is a recognized giftedness in a sought-after skill or character trait...**

asshole's giftedness fuels a climate where unproductive behavior on the part of the person is overlooked or even tolerated. The lack of accountability for poor behavior feeds the asshat's narcissism to the point where they incorrectly extend their giftedness in one area to every aspect of their life. (Eg: I'm a gifted surgeon, so I must also be gifted in administration.) If left unchallenged, this delusion of superiority grows to the point where the asshat believes they are entitled to disregard rules of social convention. While outwardly they may say, "I'm no better than anyone else," inwardly they know (believe), "No one is better than me." In some regard this is similar to what researchers have labeled as the Bathsheba Syndrome,[5] which is generally characterized by the following sequence of events:

a)   With each success the asshat becomes ever more complacent, diverting more and more attention to activities that are unproductive

b)   Each success brings increased "privileged access" to people and resources, providing thus more opportunities to engage in asinine behavior

c)   In the end, the asshat's already inflated ego is supercharged to the point where they believe social norms don't apply to them, and the asshat therefore has no problem manipulating people and events to their desired outcome.

---

[5] The Bathsheba Syndrome is derived from the biblical account of King David and Bathsheba. For me, this story is a vivid reminder that even a "man after God's own heart" can succumb to the dark sinful nature within all of us. What is most powerful is how David's heart was broken when confronted with his sin.

ASSHAT BELIEFS AND BEHAVIORS

At its core, the difference between occasionally acting like a jerk and actually being an asshat centers on a person's "beliefs" and how these beliefs influences their behavior. *The General Theory of Asshats* is based on the premise that asshats hold one of two foundational beliefs which drive their behavior. First is the belief that "Power and Influence" are the ultimate goal. Blind ambition surfaces initially in the desire to achieve success and obtain status no matter the means or costs. Abuse of power occurs once success/status is obtained and an individual is seduced by privileged access, unrestricted control over resources, and the ability to manipulate people and events towards personal gain or satisfaction.

Belief	Behavior
Their ability and skills are superior to others and therefore they are deserving of special praise and honor	• Self-centered (overly concerned for how they are seen/perceived) • Self-absorbed (regularly express and look for others to validate them publicly)
Sees (and expects) the worse in people. Believes people are bastard covered bastards with a bastard center.	• Their life motto is do unto others as they would do unto you—but do it first and completely so they can't retaliate • Regularly takes advantage of others (quick to use others as cannon fodder to advance their one self-interests)
They are the happiest when those around them are the most miserable (ideally because they caused the misery)	• Manipulative, deceitful, callous, mean, arrogant • Difficult relating to the feelings of others

The second belief that drives asshat behavior is that "belonging" to the right group is everything. The temptation to conform to peer pressure and the desire to "belong" occurs when individuals succumb to darker influences—as noted in CS Lewis' *The Inner Ring*

> I believe that in all men's lives at certain periods, and in many men's lives at all periods between infancy and extreme old age, one of the most dominant elements is the desire to be inside the local Ring and the terror of being left outside …Of all the passions, the passion for the Inner Ring is most skillful in making a man who is not yet a very bad man do very bad things." [The Inner Ring, 1944]

Why would a reasonable individual engage in mean-spirited, hateful, even torturous behavior, only to be accepted as "one of the gang"? Why risk damaging a friendship by betraying a confidence only for the prospect of creating a "special bond" centered on shared secrets? The answer centers on the motivation of belonging. Some people behave like and become asshats so that that they can stay with or join a desired social group. This is why the Stanford students playing the role of prison guard engaged in cruel treatment of prisoners (themselves fellow Stanford students)…because their fellow "guards" not only engaged in the behavior, but encouraged (even to the point of ridicule) their fellow guards to join in. We see this all the time. Why would a group of kids haze and bully a classmate—because "everyone else was doing it" and they didn't want to be left out.

The general theory of assholes can be summarized as follows:

What an asshole craves is power and influence. What they fear is being marginalized or considered insignificant. Combined, these fears and desires drive an asshole's aberrant behavior.

STORY OF AN ASSHAT: GIFTED BUT EMOTIONALLY DETACHED

Kelly is a remarkably gifted materials engineer and scientist. Because of her capabilities and experience she's often assigned to critical projects for solving the most challenging problems. In all respects she is what many organizations would define as the ideal employee—if not for her inability to work well with others.

While nearly everyone acknowledges Kelly's contributions, her personality is very abrasive and she is known to harshly criticize her colleagues' inputs and ideas. She is clearly the smartest person in the room and she knows it. She feeds off the attention senior leaders gives her which drives her to command the spotlight and never share credit with her coworkers.

Kelly seems unable to pick up on cues of common social behavior. She regularly interrupts others in meetings; when asked a question her responses are terse and abrupt. When she perceives that she is being challenged she becomes threatened and defensive. Most troubling is Kelly's inability to read emotional cues from her coworkers. Once when a colleague was expressing the emotional experience from the loss of a family member, Kelly came across as uninterested and somewhat annoyed by the distraction from important work.

The term often used to characterize Kelly's emotional detachment is *RBF*[6] (resting bitch face). The common "warning" around the water-cooler is, "Don't mess with Kelly today—she's got her RBF working full throttle." In short, Kelly appears to her coworkers as unapproachable and intimidating. No one looks forward to being on a project with Kelly.

---

[6] RBF is a colloquial term to describe someone whose facial expression occurs as disinterested or even pissed off. I reject the term. It is not a condition, syndrome or an anatomical normality to be treated with Botox. RBF is a misinformed phrase that masks a challenge with emotional self-expression. Also, RBF is nearly always associated with women, which is absolute nonsense. Challenges with emotional self-expression occur uniformly with men and women alike.

Chapter 3: Why People Behave Like Assholes—A Psychological View

In my early days in HR I would be absolutely floored by some of the shenanigans people would take part in. The things people did would make one question the future of humanity. At one point I was tempted to create a *Guide for Staying Out of HR's Dog House*, which would include tips such as:

- Never send an email to your boss or coworker when you're mad, especially if you've been drinking.
- Never share details or photos of your romantic indiscretions with coworkers,especially those who know your spouse.
- Do not use company time, resources, or property to supplement your side business, especially if the side business is illegal.
- It is never okay to stand on a conference room table and piss on a business plan you feel is worthless.
- It is never okay to pour a beer over your bosses' head, even if they are acting like a flaming asshat.

I have a close friend who works in law enforcement. We often compare stories at the end of the day to see who has encountered the biggest dumb-ass. Hearing these stories just makes you wonder why people behave the way they do. And this is especially so when dealing with workplace asshats. From a behavioral perspective it's the age-old question of nature versus nurture.[7] Are people born assholes or do they become that way over time? In truth, both nature and nurture (and also choice) come into play.

---

[7] I was the vice president of operations and technology at Amex. We were working on a complex project, and one of our directors was having trouble negotiating priorities with my counterpart in the Midwest. The director came into my office, sat down and calmly asked, "Do you have to be an asshole before you make VP here or do they send you off to asshole school?" "Well in my case," I replied, "I went to school, but I was in the advanced class."

NATURE, NURTURE, CHOICE

From the nature side, distinct asshat behaviors can be observed in children between the ages of 11 and 17 (this includes behaviors associated with narcissism and psychopathy). We likewise note that some personality traits are inherent or hardwired. For example, introversion and extraversion are traits that are believed to be part of our nature—something we are born with. We also believe we are by nature predisposed to make decisions from either our heart (based on

"Evil is knowing better but doing worse."
—The Lucifer Effect

values) or from our head (based on logic). Neither decision-making preference is better or worse than the other; they are simply different. On the other hand, there are factors associated with nurture that suggest that a large part of our behavior is learned or patterned after influential people in our lives or experiences we've had.[8] And finally, we know that some behavior is an intentional choice. Going back to Zimbardo's *The Lucifer Effect:* "Evil is knowing better but doing worse."

So, there's a three-part answer to the question, "Why do people behave like asshats?" For some, it's nature: They are hardwired toward selfish, mean-spirited behavior. For others it's nurture: Their background and experiences influence how they view and interact with the world around them. For many, though, it's simply a choice: They understand there are options for how to engage and lead people, yet they purposefully choose to give in to the dark side of the force.

---

[8] In Chapter 5: ("Dealing with Workplace Assholes"), we will discuss meme theory and how our brains pattern behaviors after what we observe in others.

PERSONALITY DISORDER VERSUS "TOXIC" BEHAVIOR

As we reflect on why do people behave like asshats, it's important to draw a distinction between a personality disorder and downright toxic behavior. A personality disorder is "an enduring pattern of inner experience and behavior that deviates markedly from the expectation of the individual's culture, is pervasive and inflexible, has an onset in adolescence or early adulthood, is stable over time, and leads to distress or impairment." The mental health field commits significant effort and resources in understanding, diagnosing, and treating personality disorders. Despite the popularity of TV personalities and pop-psychology, identifying (much less dealing with) personality disorders can only be done by qualified behavioral professionals. Yet knowing this hasn't hindered semiprofessionals and novices alike from putting people on an imaginary couch and diagnosing their behavioral problems. With this in mind I want to be clear on an important point. In this book I describe observable behaviors (more precisely personality traits) that are associated with toxic behavior in the workplace. While these behaviors are associated with personality disorders, it would be the most egregious overreach to make the leap from observed behavior to suggesting a personality disorder.

DEFINING ASSHAT BEHAVIOR—THE DARK TRIAD

In 2002 an article appeared in the *Journal of Research in Personality* that put in motion a unifying definition for asinine behavior. In the article authors Paulhus and Williams identified three distinct "socially adverse personalities" that combine to form a "Dark Triad" of deviant, aberrant, and toxic behaviors. The Dark Triad comprises narcissism, Machiavellianism and psychopathy. Since 2002 the strength of this framework for identifying and articulating asshat behavior has grown significantly. For example, a 2013 Google Scholar search for *dark triad* showed 350 citations. In 2019 the same search returned over 135,000 citations.

Since Paulus' and Williams' article in 2002, behavioral scientists and researchers have studied how the Dark Triad personality traits interact and align with better known personality disorders. A resource that aids in this effort is the Diagnostic and Statistical Manual or DSM. Published by the American Psychiatric Association, the DSM provides mental health professionals insights on symptoms and treatments for personality disorders. The DSM also outlines helpful information about statistical prevalence of disorders within the general population, gender, and age. The symptomatology for narcissism and psychopathy (antisocial) are readily defined in the DSM, while Machiavellianism is linked to paranoia behaviors. Using the DSM and studies on the Dark Triad, let's consider the observed behaviors associated with each of these personality disorders.

Narcissism

Dark Triad Trait	Summary Description	Clinical Definition
Narcissism	Unusually self-confident, unwilling to admit mistakes or listen to advice, unable to learn from experiences	Grandiose sense of self-importance and entitlement, arrogant behaviors and attitude

Of the three personalities in the Dark Triad, narcissism is the easiest to recognize and what we most often discuss. The reason we can readily identify a narcissist is because many of us have similar selfish tendencies. We are given to embellish our resume and using hyperbole when recounting our accomplishments. Notable personality traits of narcissism are:

- Exaggerated self-image and self-appraisal (over inflated ego)
- Holding others to unrealistic expectations while their own standards are remarkably low

- Entitled, self-centered, condescending
- Seeking and expecting to be recognized as superior/noteworthy.
- Requiring excessive admiration—looks to be lauded by others; surrounds themselves with yes men (people who will say what they want to hear)
- Takes advantage of others to achieve their own gain

In the workplace, narcissists will ensure their accomplishments and maintain their dominance by routinely playing down the contributions of others. Narcissists will also make it a point to keep the spotlight on others' failures, often long past the event (e.g., Don't forget that major mistake Charlie made seven years ago on the XYZ contract). Also, it is not beyond the narcissists to take undue credit for others' accomplishments or even set up someone to fail so they can step in and save the day.

A narcissist's ego inhibits them from accepting any critical feedback. In fact, if any personal shortcoming is pointed out, they will be quick to deflect to someone else that they feel is worse than them. Thus, for a narcissist, their status (power and influence) is their strength and feedback their kryptonite. A narcissist will protect their status at all costs. When attending social gatherings, it's critical for the narcissist to "see and be seen" with high-power/high-profile people.

While on the surface it may appear that narcissists are well-connected, in truth they have a very shallow social network. Narcissists have many acquaintances but few, if any, real friends. This is why for many of them the thought of retiring is terrifying; they know all too well that retiring is akin to abdicating the throne. In retirement, narcissists can be some of the loneliest people in the world.

Machiavellianism

Dark Triad Trait	Summary Description	Clinical Definition
Machiavellianism (Paranoid)	Cynical, distrustful, overly sensitive to criticism, skeptical of others true intentions	Distrustful and suspicious of others, motives of others are seen as negative

Of all the Dark Triad adverse personalities, Machiavellianism "is the most likely of the three to be modified by experience." Machiavellianism is often characterized along a continuum from low to high. Low-Machs possess an "unconventional view of morality, a willingness to manipulate, lie to, and exploit others, and focus exclusively on their own goals and agendas." High-Machs are in essence low-Machs on steroids; they are "exceedingly willing to manipulate others and take a certain pleasure in successfully deceiving others."

As noted earlier, Machiavellianism is closely linked to paranoia behaviors and therefore can exhibit several of the following personality traits:

- Suspects without sufficient basis that others are exploiting, harming, or deceiving them
- Preoccupied with unjustified doubts about the loyalty or trustworthiness of others
- Is reluctant to confide in others because of unwarranted fear that the information will be used maliciously against them
- Persistently bears grudges (has a mental enemies list and is calculating in exacting retribution)
- Quick to perceive attacks on their character or reputation that are not apparent to others, and reacts aggressively and angrily in order to counterattack

Perhaps the single best word to define Machiavellianism is political. Both low and high Machiavellians are gifted at using their personal charisma to form self-serving political alliances. One way to accomplish this is to demand absolute loyalty from their direct reports. Heaven help the poor soul who fails to kiss the ring of the Machiavellian king/queen. They will forever be on the "enemy of the state" watch list. It is the most fascinating thing to watch the power play when a high-Mach leaves an organization. The Machiavellian leader will work the system to help ensure those who were the most loyal receive high praise, promotions, and advancements. However, those who ended up on the enemy list receive harsh criticism as the high-Mach sows seeds of doubt and uncertainty among the remaining leaders. Those most unfortunate are the countless minions who faithfully kissed the Mach's backside but were little more than cannon fodder in service of the Mach's self-centered ambitions. Once the Mach is gone, these poor minions realize they've burned too many bridges in service to their Mach overlord. Without the political cover of their Mach overlord they have few options. Some will choose to "retire-in-place," while others will opt to exit the organization. Some minions will even look to follow the Mach to their next job.

Psychopathy

Dark Triad Trait	Summary Description	Clinical Definition
Psychopathy (Antisocial)	Risk taker, enjoys testing the limits	Disregard for the truth, impulsive, fail to conform to social norms

Psychopathy is the most unsettling of the adverse personalities of the Dark Triad because we often connect psychopaths with the worse of the human condition: evil and heinous acts of violence of man against man. Key personality traits of psychopathy are:

- Self-esteem derived from personal gain, power, or pleasure
- Failure to conform to lawful or culturally normative ethical behavior
- Manipulative: frequent use of subterfuge to influence or control others; readily uses seduction, charm, glibness or ingratiation to achieve one's end
- Deceitfulness: dishonest and fraudulent; misrepresentation of own contributions or accomplishments; embellishment or fabrication when relating events
- Callousness: lack of concern for feelings of others; lack of guilt or remorse about the negative or harmful effects of one's actions on others; aggressive; sadism
- Hostility: persistent or frequent angry feelings; anger or irritability in response to minor slights and insults; mean, nasty, or vengeful behavior
- Irresponsibility: disregard for and failure to honor financial and other obligations or commitments; lack of respect for and lack of follow through on agreements and promises
- Impulsivity: acting on the spur of the moment in response to immediate stimuli; acting on a momentary basis without a plan or consideration of outcomes; difficulty establishing and following plans
- Risk-taking: engagement in dangerous, risky, and potentially self-damaging activities, unnecessarily and without regard for consequences; boredom proneness and thoughtless initiation of activities to counter boredom; lack of concern for one's limitations and denial of the reality of personal danger

In organizations, psychopaths at high levels of influence often create a constant litany of lawsuits for unfair business or labor practices. They frequently fail to comply with agreed-upon terms and conditions, seeing themselves as shrewd negotiators versus someone who reneges on personal commitments. Thus, psychopaths are masters of deceit, lying with ease and conning the most vulnerable. They are quick to agree on conditions favorable to the other party because they have no intention of complying with the agreement. Observing psychopaths at work is like watching an episode of "Survivor," as temporary alliances are built and short-term gains offered in order to compel others towards favorable actions.

Psychopaths at work can become verbally abusive and physically intimidating. This is especially so if they perceive any threat to their power or influence. If threatened, the psychopath will respond with exponential force to the perceived threat. If a business deal turns sour, the psychopath will abruptly and irresponsibly break their commitments (financially or otherwise) and assess blame anywhere but on them.

Overlap within the Dark Triad

To be clear, narcissism, Machiavellianism, and psychopathy are distinct personality traits all their own. An individual displaying any one of these traits will be very difficult to work with or for. However, within the Dark Triad framework the three personality traits overlap, as noted in the original 2002 article by Paulus and Williams:

> Despite their diverse origins, the personalities composing this "Dark Triad" share a number of features. To varying degrees, all three entail a socially malevolent character with behavior tendencies toward self-promotion, emotional coldness, duplicity, and aggressiveness. As a result, there is now empirical evidence for the overlap of Machiavellianism with psychopathy; for narcissism with psychopathy and with Machiavellianism with narcissism.

As it relates to workplace assholes there are important points to keep in mind: (a) Not every asshat will display every personality trait associated with narcissism, Machiavellianism, and psychopathy. Some may have a stronger disposition to narcissism or Machiavellianism and less to psychopathy traits; (b) when combined, narcissism,

Machiavellianism, and psychopathy reflect a force multiplier that rapidly moves an individual from an annoying jerk to a flaming asshole.

Chapter 4: The Neuroscience of Why People Behave Like Assholes

With the Dark Triad framework we have a psychological perspective to help us understand why people behave like assholes. Now we will consider the neuroscience behind asinine behavior.

Here is a vastly oversimplified distinction between psychology and neuroscience. Psychology is the study of the mind. Neuroscience is the study of the brain. At first glance this may seem like semantics, but there is a subtle difference. When we study the mind via psychology, what we are seeking to understand is the how and why people think what they do. A more descriptive terminology would be metacognition: the thinking about thinking. From a psychological perspective we try to understand how a person's experiences, preferences, and personality influence how they think and, in turn, how this affects how they behave.

Neuroscience looks to build our understanding for the how and why our brain functions. More specifically, neuroscience draws our attention to the neurology (wiring) in our brains and attempts to map this wiring for clues about which areas of our brain influence specific behaviors. For example, we now understand that the part of our brain that lights up when we hit our thumb with a hammer is the same part of our brain that fires off when we feel excluded. So when someone shares that they feel physically hurt when they are ostracized by their peer group, we have a better understanding why that is.[9]

For our purposes, we will consider the neuroscience of asshat behavior in three areas: empathy, connectedness, and self-awareness.

---

[9] To be frank, the distinction between psychology and neuroscience is becoming increasingly harder to define. The positive effect of an ever-increasing focus on brain science has been a multidisciplinary approach to the study of human behavior. In fact, many grad students have the option of pursuing dual degrees in psychology and neuroscience.

LACK OF EMPATHY

Earlier, I discussed whether people are assholes by nature, nurture, or choice. This debate is a throwback to the age-old philosophical question, "Are people inherently good or naturally bad?" In my view, we are by nature bad; or, more to the point, we are by nature egocentric, thinking more of ourselves than of others. If you want observable evidence of this, just sit and watch little kids at play and you'll easily see our "bad nature" emerges. In some regard self-centeredness is a preservation mechanism. Yet we know instinctively that we need a group for protection and support. While our brain wiring causes us to be selfish by nature, there's likewise wiring in our brains that serves as a counterbalance by influencing empathy and compassion. The empathy wiring helps explain why we feel guilty when we are overly selfish and how we are moved to put the needs of others ahead of our own desires. It's as if there's a tug-of-war inside our heads.[10]

We are by nature bad; or, more to the point, we are by nature egocentric; thinking more of ourselves than of others.

In 2013 researchers Silani, Lamm, Ruff and Singer published a paper in the *Journal of Neuroscience* outlining a behavioral experiment designed to better understand the interplay within our brains between our natural egocentric behavior and the brain's capacity to move us towards empathy. The premise for this experiment was that humans tend to use themselves as a reference point to judge others. The technical term is called *egocentric emotional bias* (EEB), and it refers to our tendency to project our own mental state on to others. For example, if you're having a great day, your tendency is to expect everyone else is having a great day. Or if you're having a rotten day, you expect that everyone else must be having the same.

---

[10] Think of the cartoon where the main character is struggling with a moral dilemma and suddenly an angel and a devil appear, one on each shoulder.

What this experiment discovered is fascinating. We can readily identify with the emotions of others if one of two conditions exist: Either we are (a) in a "neutral state," neither floating on a cloud or wallowing in the dumps, or (b) we encounter someone who is in the same place that we are. If neither condition exists, the researchers discovered that a specific part of our brain kicks in to pull us out of our EEB and fire-up our capacity for empathy. This part of our brain is the right *supramarginal gyrus* (rSMG).

Additionally, the study found that when the rSmg is impaired the ability to be empathic is diminished. In people with a psychopathy disorder, their rSMG fails to become active when imagining the pain that others might be feeling. More alarming is that researchers found when psychopaths imagined the pain occurring in others, the activity in their ventral striatum, the part of the brain associated with pleasure, increases. The bottom line is not only are psychopaths unable to relate to the pain that others encounter, but also, to varying degrees, they actually take pleasure in it.

> **The bottom line is not only are psychopaths unable to relate to the pain that others encounter, but also, to varying degrees, they actually take pleasure in it.**

So while the brains of most of us are wired to balance egocentric emotional bias (selfishness) with empathy; workplace assholes "shut-off" their empathy for others, and the worst ones take some measure of pleasure in causing misery for others.

LACK OF CONNECTEDNESS

Earlier I mentioned that an asshat will have many acquaintances but few "real" friends. I came to this conclusion many years ago when I was coaching a senior executive who was nearing retirement. Most executives realize that when they retire, their sphere of influence will lessen. For asshats, however, even their social connections diminish significantly when they retire. The executive I was coaching was notably anxious about retiring because all of his social connections revolved around work. As it turned out, his concerns were well founded. I caught up with him several months after he retired, and I could readily observe that he was a different person. Gone was the rough, emboldened demeanor. His physical stature had likewise changed: He was sullen and a bit disheveled. A few minutes into our visit he confided that the loss of status and influence since retiring was difficult, but what was the most unsettling was the lack of social connection since leaving his company. Outside of family ties (which mainly centered on his spouse), he had very little interaction with people. He was, in his own words, remarkably lonely.[11]

The human brain is wired for group living and we are drawn to hang out with those with whom we have an affinity. Our brains perceive disconnections to our social circles in the same manner we perceive a physical threat; our "sympathetic nervous system and hypothalamic-pituitary-adrenal axis goes into overdrive, increasing inflammation and compromising the immune system".

Yet the very nature of the Dark Triad (narcissism, Machiavellianism, and psychopathy) creates the conditions where assholes lack any real or meaningful social connections. The selfishness of a narcissist is hardly a character trait for attracting friends. Nor will the suspicious and devious nature of Machiavellianism entice deep friendships. What more can be said about the antisocial disposition of psychopathy?

Once the power and influence of an asshat are gone, the few connections they did have vanish as well. The lack of connectedness can become especially difficult for them because no matter how big a jerk you are at some point in your life you will

---

[11] In later chapters I highlight how disconnected we all seem to be. There was a time when folks could name four or five really good friends. Now, we can barely name one. To further make this point consider that in January 2018 Britain announced the creation of a new position: "Minister of Loneliness." In establishing this new position, Prime Minister Theresa May stated, "For far too many people, loneliness is the sad reality of modern life." The announcement cited the statistic that more than 9 million people always or often feel lonely in the U.K.

need people who care about you. You need to feel as if you belong, that you matter to someone.

The neuroscience of belonging is fascinating. In *Your Brain at Work* David Rock crafts a threat/reward model to describe how our brains deal with various social interactions. Rock's model focuses on status, certainty, autonomy, relatedness and fairness (SCARF). It is with respect to relatedness that we can visualize how asshats often burn bridges that most people would use to create meaningful connections. As an illustration, Rock uses the "identification friend or foe" (IFF) system used within military and civil applications for distinguishing friendly vehicles, forces, and aircrafts. Developed in the 1930s by the U.S. Naval Research Labs, IFF was a radio system that could not only detect targets on the ground, sea, or in the air but also distinguish if the target was friendly or hostile: a capability that was quite handy for planes returning to carriers under poor visibility.

From a neuroscience perspective our brains are likewise wired to distinguish between friend and foe. However, assholes reconfigure IFF (identify **friend** or foe) to IMF (identify **minion** or foe). This is because friends are those for whom we perceive to be most like us. The Dark Triad nature of asshats is such that they rarely see anyone as their peer or equal.

Asshats reconfigure IFF (identify friend or foe) to IMF (identify minion or foe).

Likewise, asshats adhere to the Machiavellian philosophy that, "it's better to be feared than respected." To quote from Machiavelli's *The Prince:*

> "[On] the question of being feared or loved, I come to the conclusion that, men loving according to their own and fearing according to that of the prince, a wise prince should establish himself on that which is in his own control and not in that of others." Machiavelli continues, "men have less scruple in offending one who is beloved than one who is feared, for love is preserved

by the link of obligation which, owing to the baseness of men, is broken at every opportunity for their advantage; but fear preserves you by dread of punishment which never fails."

SELF-AWARE BUT DON'T CARE

The final neuroscience view of asshole behavior that we'll look at is self-awareness. In the appendix ("Are You an Asshole?") I'll consider the question, "Can an asshole change?" But the questions behind the question are, "Do you know you're an asshole?" and "Do you care?" The last one centers on our capacity for self-awareness, and empathy.

Most of us are familiar with the idea of IQ (or intelligence quotient). IQ is a relative/comparative measure of a person's intelligence based on their responses to standard tests. What you may not know is that a person's IQ typically tops out between the ages 16 and 20. In other words, around the time we reach our twenties we are about as intelligent as we are ever going to be (let that soak in a minute, especially if you have teenage kids).

The good news is that our IQ is only part of what contributes to our success. What's more influential in work and life is what we call our *emotional intelligence* (commonly referred to as *EQ*). EQ is a set of emotional and social skills that collectively establish how well we perceive and express ourselves, develop and maintain social relationships, cope with challenges, and use emotional information in an effective and meaningful way. Interestingly, unlike IQ, which tops out around age 20, our EQ never stops developing as our brains continuously grow new neural fibers that enable us to draw meaning from the experiences we encounter.

A key facet of EQ is emotional self-awareness: defined as the ability to not only recognize but also to understand how our own emotions impact us and those around us. From a neuroscience perspective, self-awareness provides the information essential for conscious self-monitoring and adapting our behavior in light of our experiences. Our brain wiring depends on self-awareness for learning by conscious experience, not only within ourselves but also between individuals.

The neuroscience of self-awareness is most evident when working with individuals recovering from traumatic brain injury (TBI), as neuroscientists have observed a breakdown of functional interactions between nodes within the frontal-parietal control network.

Assholes regularly struggle with self-awareness. They seem oblivious (or worse indifferent) to how their behavior adversely impacts others. They often talk over others, especially those in lower level positions. Asshats are more focused on being interesting than on being interested. Whether as a result of faulty brain wiring or a behavioral disorder, assholes function in a state of unconsciousness. And this extends beyond work to their home/family lives.

The fundamental question goes back to motivation: Why does someone behave the way they do? For example, within each of us is the desire for influence: to be noteworthy in our contributions and recognized for our impact. This desire for influence is neither a good or bad motive. The motive for influence moves from normal to asshole when fueled by aggressive, self-centered, and self-serving intents.

Chapter 5: Attraction, Cultural Influences And Organizational Impact

There are several factors that contribute to people acting badly in organizations.

THE APPEAL OF THE DARK TRIAD

There is a certain charisma that embodies those who give themselves over to the Dark Triad of narcissism, Machiavellianism, and psychopathy. A close friend of mine is a senior official with a national law enforcement agency. They share how the very best criminals have a distinguishable charm that causes people to let down their defenses. Then, before a victim knows what happened, the criminal has hustled them out of their life's savings (or worse).

There is likewise an allure of the Dark Triad as a means to advance one's political or career goals. In fact, there is evidence that being an a-hole can actually help a person climb the corporate ladder. One reason people behave badly is they observe how well this works for other's success. Dr. Robert Hogan emphasizes this point when he notes that while dark traits help people "get ahead" in the workplace, the dark traits fight against "getting along" with others. This helps explain why a notable percentage of "high flyers" in an organization may have more talent for politics than for leadership.

Consider this historical footnote: In a study of over three dozen U.S. Presidents, ratings of Machiavellianism were positively associated with not only charisma but also overall performance. Machiavellian presidents also tended to serve more years in elected office and have a greater number of legislative achievements. Moreover, the success of Machiavellian leaders was significantly enhanced when paired with higher levels of intelligence. It would seem that the combination of intelligence and self-serving cunning can lead to great success and even greater toxicity in the work environment.

In the corporate world, narcissistic CEOs tend to favor grandiose, headline-grabbing actions. There was even a phrase coined to memorialize this: *big hairy audacious goal*. BHAGs can have large consequences, which can be positive or negative: big wins or big losses. However, business results emerging from firms with narcissistic CEOs often perform in extreme and fluctuating manners. What's most interesting is this: When results are positive the narcissistic CEO is quick to take credit, and when the results are poor, the same CEO deflects blame. This makes for interesting reading of their annual reports. What I find most alarming is that evolutionary psychologists have theorized that some organizational leaders are motivated towards extreme risk-taking behavior (in spite of potential dangers) because of the potential upside for their personal success, especially under benevolent circumstances or in the face of weak opposition.

Since his passing, there have been several books and movies written about Steve Jobs and Apple. By pure business metrics, Apple is one of the most successful companies of all time. For example, in August 2018 Apple became the first publicly traded U.S. company to reach a market cap of $1 trillion. Yet when you hear the stories of how Jobs interacted with the people in his life, his company, and the business world, it seems clear that his behavior aligned with that of a flaming asshole. Now there are those who make the argument that his approach to leading is what made Apple successful—their point being that the only way for the company to achieve what it did was by Jobs' hateful, intimidating mean-spiritedness. I reject this notion completely. Perhaps the question should be, "How much greater would Apple be today had Jobs not been so asinine?" This should motivate us to define a clear and concise definition of effective leadership: leadership that ensures achieving desired results, while sustaining and guarding the well-being of valuable resources (such as people and nature). What good is it to be the world's greatest builder if the cost is clear-cutting old-growth forests? Or what value is there in achieving record profits if you chew up your employees in the process?

SOCIAL AND CULTURAL INFLUENCES

In *The Narcissism Epidemic*, authors Twenge and Campbell point to an alarming shift towards a more self-centered culture. As evidence, they point to the motivation given for volunteering to help charities and advance social causes. There was a time not long ago, when people gave their time and energy to those in need because it was the right thing to do. However, when you ask a volunteer today why they donate their time and effort the typical response is: "Because it makes me feel good." While subtle, there is an important distinction to consider.

What's the difference between a motive to volunteer that's driven by a "moral compass to help those in need" versus "feeling good about giving time to those less fortunate?" Clearly helping those in need should cause us to feel good. But if the "feeling" is absent, will the volunteering continue?

Yet we need not fear altruism has totally vanished. Consider this story. For a while I lived in a part of the U.S. that's prone to major storms and tornados. After a large storm, volunteers were asked to walk a large field where debris from several homes had been deposited. The homeowners were hopeful to recover a few of the treasures they lost. About fifty of us walked shoulder to shoulder over the field, stopping along the way to sift through countless remnants of what used to be someone's home. A few yards from me a searcher came across a bundle of baseball cards. We gathered around and inspected the cards. Someone noted the cards were current players and most likely not of significant monetary value. But one of the searchers countered, "Well they're important to the person who collected them." We all stood there for a few seconds and then got down on our hands and knees and searched for more cards. After a few minutes we found several more bundles of cards. We later found out that when the cards were returned to their young owner, it was one of the most emotional reunions that afternoon.

Unfortunately, the story above is all too rare. Without question we are living in the "selfie" generation. While flying to Chicago I endured what seemed to be an eternity as the young person beside me took dozens of selfies before finding one suitable to send to their friend. Watching this in-flight photoshoot, I was both amused and concerned. I recalled how psychologists have noted that 80% of the time young people are on social media they are either talking about themselves or posting selfies. These same researchers have noted a connection between narcissistic social-media usage and a decrease in empathy and self-regard.

It should be no surprise that the rise in selfie-narcissism has spawned a loss in common civility. More and more people are so focused on their own needs and interests that the concerns of others are ignored. This can be readily observed but how many people blow through traffic lights on purpose. It's as if they're saying, "My time is more important than yours."

ASSHATS IMPACT ON ORGANIZATIONS

Throughout history the world has witnessed the devastating effect of ruthless dictators and belligerent leaders. When we study these people we clearly see all three of the Dark Triad traits at work. Maniacs such as Gadhafi, Saddam, or Bin Laden are examples. Their psychopathy provoked extreme brutality, and their Machiavellianism facilitated strategic manipulation, while their narcissistic tendencies fueled a sense of superiority.

Closer to home we can likewise observe the impact of ass-clowns within organizations. Below are just a few:

- While narcissists often use soft manipulation tactics, psychopaths go with hard (in-your-face) tactics. Machs will go either way, depending on the need and their mood.

- In academic settings, psychopaths readily copy exams, whereas Machs are quick to plagiarize. And in situations for extra credit or team projects, psychopaths and Machs exploit loopholes in the system to claim credit for accomplishments they did not achieve. This behavior extends readily in the corporate world.

- Psychopaths respond aggressively to physical threats, while narcissists require a significant ego-threat before they respond. Machs are more cautious and deliberate in their behavior: Hence they do not act on temptation like psychopaths. When ego-depleted however, Machs act out like psychopaths.

- Research bears out a robust relationship between Machs and unethical decision-making.

- Narcissists claim to be very creative; however their creative performance is no better than anyone else's. Although narcissists are skilled in convincing others to see their ideas as "best," it is clear that toxic leaders have a negative impact on the creative activities of others.

- Narcissists characterized by chronic overconfidence will be less likely to accept constructive feedback and may even be dismissive of it all together.

- Machs are more skilled and more willing to engage in faking employee interviews, while narcissists are effective at making good first impression, but this quickly wears off once folks see the asshole beneath the surface.

- The core traits of psychopaths—coldness, lack of empathy, self-centeredness, ruthlessness—makes them some of the most financially successful business people in the world. Psychopaths find it easy to manipulate people, and their predatory nature allows them to lie convincingly.

Chapter 6: Assholes in the Workplace

While writing this book I constantly bounced back and forth between two worlds: the behavioral science world that wants to understand why someone acts like an asshole *and* the HR world that is dedicated to creating a workplace in which people thrive professionally and personally. Whenever I mention the concept of organizational proctology, people are genuinely fascinated with the behavioral aspect of asshats. The psychology and neuroscience dimensions of human behavior are indeed very interesting and at times can be entertaining. But, without fail, the conversation about people acting badly in the workplace always circles back to one key question: "What do I do about the asshole in *my* life?" If you're in a place where you're confronted with one at work, or if someone you deeply care for is suffering because of a one at work, the only question that really matters is: "How do I make this madness stop? Please!"

As much as I wish there were a straightforward three-step plan for dealing with assholes in the workplace, the simple truth is that there are no easy answers. Regrettably there are no laws prohibiting people from behaving in an asinine manner. And while many organizations have code-of-conduct statements, I have yet to see an organization publish a formal "anti-asshole position."[12]

Although there are no *easy* answers, there are answers for dealing with assholes in the workplace. The reason I chose to frame this book as "field notes" is to provide context for simplifying answers to the very complex question: "How do I deal with a person behaving badly at work?" To this end, I offer chapters 6, 7, and—especially—8.

Let me mention here that the impact on a person's mental and physical health from a workplace asshole is remarkably similar to the impact of an abusive relationship. So much so that early on in the development of this book, I gave considerable thought to drawing on this comparison. While the impacts have similarities, they are very, very different. I would never want to mischaracterize the trauma associated

---

[12] Notwithstanding policies on bullying and harassment, which we will discuss later.

with being in an abusive relationship as equivalent to the hardships of dealing with a workplace asshole.

Still, let me be clear on a very important point. If you or someone you care about is working with or for an asshole, you are not stuck. There are many good and compelling options you can consider. Also, you are not alone. You do have people in your corner. And most assuredly, there are brighter days ahead. But above all, please know this: There is no reason whatsoever anyone should have to tolerate, survive, or endure an asshole in the workplace!

CAUTION: HEALTH HAZARD: ASSHOLE-RELATED-STRESS (ARSE)

As noted at the beginning of this book, there's an epidemic in the workplace that is creating alarming physical ailments such as chronic headaches, muscle tension, fatigue, and issues regulating both sleep and eating. The epidemic is likewise spawning psychological concerns such as reduced aspiration, diminished sense of confidence, depression, anxiety, and emotional detachment. I've named the epidemic *asshole-related-stress* (ARSe). Working for (or with) an asshole can be one of the most stressful experiences of your professional life, and the impact from ARSe lingers long after the asshole is out of a person's life. When I work with people who've experienced ARSe, –their just recalling the memory triggers a visceral reaction. A friend who was recovering from ARSe explained it this way:

Things were so bad at work that my only defense was to hang on until Friday afternoon, with the prospect of an asshole-free weekend. But the relief was short-lived. Somewhere around Sunday afternoon the reality of having to go back to work the next day hit me, and I was overwhelmed knowing that within a few hours I'd be right back in the mire. And I became physically ill.

Even now, after that asshole is long gone, I still find myself sometimes looking at the clock Sunday afternoons and I flashback to where I was years ago, and I break out in to a cold sweat.

ARSe is a virus, but not a virus like the flu. ARSe is a *"mind-virus"* that erodes the self-confidence of those it infects. It occurs everywhere–at home, at work, in school, in social groups. Wherever people form teams and collectives, there

ARSe is a "mind-virus" that erodes the self-confidence of those it infects.

will always be assholes. For the purpose of this book we'll focus on ARSe in the workplace, which I define as follows:

ARSe occurs in the workplace when a person sees no way out of miserable interactions with a boss or a co-worker. These interactions encompass unrelenting demands, demeaning behavior, disrespect and general disregard for common workplace civility—all of which continue for seemingly interminable periods of time. Simultaneously contending with these interactions is the belief that there is little awareness, concern or interest by the organization to intervene and resolve the situation.[13]

As I interact with HR leaders from around the world, concern for stress in the workplace is on everyone's radar. At a health-care conference an HR leader shared a story of reviewing annual medical costs with their insurance provider. There was good news and bad news. The bad news was a disturbing trend showing an increase in stress-related interventions (such as medications and counseling). The "good" news was the upward trend was being experienced by nearly every organization across the U.S.

According to a joint study by National Public Radio, The Robert Wood Johnson Foundation, and the Harvard School of Public Health, "problems at work" ranked third as causes of stress, surpassed only by illness or the death of a loved one. The evidence connecting workplace ARSe and health is widespread.

---

[13] My definition of ARSe is an adaptation of the American Psychological Association's description of chronic stress.

Consider the following articles:

- "Is Your Boss Making You Sick" in the *Washington Post*, October 2014, noting the connection between dealing with a bad boss and increased risk of heart attacks.

- "How A Bad Boss Can Make You Sick" in *Forbes*, October 2014, noting a Keas study that "found that 77% of employees experienced physical symptoms of stress from bad bosses" with "60% (of employees) more likely to suffer heart trauma."

- "Bad Bosses Can Be Bad For Your Health" in *USA Today*, August 2012, outlining presentation given at American Psychiatric Association that pointed out that "75% of working adults say the worst aspect of their job—the most stressful aspect of their job—is their immediate boss...[creating] enormous health costs and are a major source of misery for many people."

- "How to Deal With a Toxic Coworker" in *Fortune*, July 2015, Noting survey in which "four out of five employees either work now or have worked in the past with a colleague whose passive aggressiveness, negativity, habit of blaming others, or spreading malicious rumors has thrown the whole team's morale—and productivity—under the bus."

- "How To Deal With Toxic Coworkers—And Keep Your Sanity In Check" in *FastCompany*, September 2014, spelling out how "toxic" coworkers "not only breed a pessimistic work environment, but can negatively impact productivity and decision-making."

The long-term impact of ARSe is unmistakable as a continuous cycle of stress creates havoc mentally, physically, and socially. The Mayo Clinic helps frame our understanding of the impact of stress on our body, our mood, and our behavior.

Impact of Stress		
On Body	*On Mood*	*On Behavior*
• Headache • Muscle tension or pain • Chest pain • Fatigue • Change in sex drive • Stomach upset • Sleep problems	• Anxiety • Restlessness • Lack of motivation or focus • Irritability or anger • Sadness or depression • Diminished interest in intimacy	• Overeating or undereating • Angry outbursts • Drug or alcohol abuse • Tobacco use • Social withdrawal

When the brain is forced into a constant-crisis mode, our stress hormones push us into an adrenalized fight-or-flight state. Research has shown that while certain levels of stress and recovery are good physiologically, prolonged cycles of stress eventually lead to exhaustion and ineffectiveness because our bodies react poorly when overexerted without rest. Just as concerning as the mental and physical impact, ARSe has devastating impacts socially as the fabric of trust breaks down between people, teams and even within the organization as a whole.

The pressure to achieve greater results with fewer resources is difficult enough without the added burden of dealing with workplace assholes. Unfortunately, there seems to be no end to them in the workplace.

PREVALENCE OF ASSHOLES IN THE WORKPLACE

Encounters with workplace a-holes occur with such regularity that most employees have come to accept them as part of their everyday work-life. Yet some employees are confounded by the prevalence of them in the workplace, often wondering aloud, "Is it just me or does it seem like we're surrounded by assholes?" Take comfort, it's not you. Organizational climate research from 1950 through 1990 found that 60 to 75% of employees identified their immediate boss as the worst aspect of their job; in 2010 nearly 60% of employees noted their boss had exhibited destructive leadership behaviors. More recent data shows the vast majority of job seekers cite a bad boss as the reason they are looking for a new job.

According to Dr. Sutton with Harvard University, "We are surrounded by assholes." Citing a number of academic studies as well as anecdotal evidence on difficult people in the workplace, Sutton draws several interesting conclusions:

- 80/20 rule: 80% of workplace assholes are bosses/20% are co-workers
- The higher an asshat is in the organization–the greater their asinine behavior

To gain a sense of how often we find asshats in the workplace, let's consider the following questions: (a) What is the prevalence of bad actors in the general population and by extension in the general workforce? (b) What is the frequency of workplace asshats as you go up the corporate ladder?

Recall from chapter 3 that there are three distinct character traits of the Dark Triad of asinine behavior: narcissism (selfishness and feelings of superiority), Machiavellianism (expecting the worse in people and an unprincipled manipulation of others to achieve self-serving gains), and psychopathy (satisfaction in the disregard and violation of the rights of others). Research suggests that these three traits overlap, but in order to help us discern the frequency of assholes in the workplace, we'll start by looking at each trait separately. Let's begin with psychopathy.

How many psychopaths are there in the workplace? According to the DSM, within the general population, the frequency of people with a psychopathic personality disorder is between 0.2% and 3.3%. There are tons of factors that go into this figure and behaviorists, clinicians and researchers spend countless hours considering this data. For our purposes, and in the simplest terms possible, we'll say the overall prevalence of psychopathy in the general workplace is roughly 1%. So, if we have a thousand people in the room (big room), ten could possibly be psychopaths. This point is made with great effect in a 2012 TED talk in which Jon Ronson suggests that while the occurrence of psychopathy in the general population is 1%, this increases to 4% among CEOs and business leaders. (I bet you slept better not knowing this!)

So how many narcissists are there in the workplace? Again, according to the DSM, the prevalence of narcissism in the general population is between 0% and 6%. However, within the general workplace, I would conservatively estimate the prevalence of narcissism to be on the high side of this range. If you want to validate this, just ask any HR person to summarize the type of employee-relations issues they deal with on a regular basis. Without question "selfishness" will surface as a root cause. Then ask your HR friend to summarize issues they often encounter with senior leaders and "superiority complex" will emerge as a theme. Based on my experience, I would say narcissism ranges from 4% within the general workforce to as high as 12% within executive ranks.

And then there is Machiavellianism, those who expect the worst from their fellow-man, while manipulating them in order to achieve self-serving gains. An often-used synonym for Machiavellianism is *being political*. Frankly, we could stop here and accept the widely held belief that organizations are one big political circus. The plain truth is political savviness is a critical skill we all would do well to master; but political savviness is like "the Force": There is a "light side" and a "dark side." Let's press on with our question. How prevalent is Machiavellianism in the workplace? Two observations can help with this answer.

First, how often and where do you see employees aligned around a single person, be that a boss or a coworker? Workplace assholes use the dark side of "the political force" to establish alliances based on absolute loyalty. These political alliances resemble the corporate version of street gangs—a bit more sophisticated and less overtly violent but just as ruthless and self-serving. More often than not, these alliances form around bosses, and the strongest alliances form around those leaders at the highest levels. To be clear, there are occasions in which asshole coworkers engage in bullying and intimidation so as to demand a gang like loyalty from those in their workgroup.

Our second observation for Machiavellianism centers on how the lack of political savviness creates a hurdle in someone's career. The HR term used in this case is *derailer,* and it refers to a deficiency or misstep that short-circuited someone's career. Research shows that the lack of political savviness has a much greater potential to derail the career of business-unit leaders and senior

These observations on Machiavellianism reinforce an awareness that more assholes are seen at the executive ranks than lower in the organization.

executives than nearly any other level in an organization. I've never met a senior leader who didn't understand the importance of political savviness in managing their career, but to the asshole this insight fuels their Machiavellian nature. Combined, these observations on Machiavellianism reinforce an awareness that more assholes are seen in the executive ranks than lower in the organization.

To get to a quantified percentage of Machiavellianism in the workplace, Drs. Campbell and Miller give us a hand by highlighting that both Machiavellianism and psychopathy are substantially correlated with scores for narcissism. Meaning that as the percentage of one trait goes up or down, the percentage of the other traits increase or decrease accordingly. Using the prevalence of narcissism as the baseline, we can align the percentage of Machiavellianism to likewise range from 4% within the general workforce to as high as 12% within executive ranks.

Let me summarize what I believe to be occurring in the workplace.

- The prevalence of psychopathy in the general workplace is 1% and increases to 4% at executive ranks.
- While the prevalence of narcissism in the general population is between 0% and 6%, experience suggests that within the

workplace narcissism ranges from 4% generally to 12% at executive ranks.
- If we align Machiavellianism and narcissism we would also expect a range of 4% generally and 12% at executive ranks.

Combining these insights and my experience in HR, I've come to the conclusion that at the general workforce level the prevalence of assholes is 4% and increases to 12% as you get to the executive level.

Prevalence of Assholes in workplace

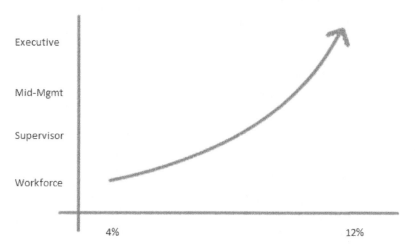

It may be somewhat comforting to know that if you're struggling with an a-hole at work you are not alone. That said, it still sucks to work with a jerk.

IMPACT AN ASS-CLOWN "BOSS" HAS ON PERFORMANCE

At times, individuals suffering from ARSe can mask their diminished mental and physical distress while maintaining a moderate level of performance, but the impact of ARSe on team performance is not as easy to mask. When a team is faced with an asshole boss, the impact to performance unfolds in a sequence of events that typically evolve as follows:

Phase 1: The "What Just Happened?" Moment

If the asshole boss is an unknown, someone brand-new to the organization, there will a honeymoon period during which everything is puppies and unicorns. Soon however, with very little warning, the first signs of asinine behavior emerge. This may occur in a team setting or in a one-on-one meeting. The behavior can surface as an unrealistic demand (e.g., "I need you to pick up my dry cleaning") or a backhanded put down (e.g., "So, this is what passes for acceptable performance around here"). More likely the bad behavior will be something that asserts the boss's position of dominance (scheduling over preexisting meetings or insisting that all meetings are held in their office). Here are a few real-life stories.

Commissioner Gordon *(e.g., taking credit).*

An employee was on a business trip with their new boss. The boss wanted to do a road show to see their territory and press the flesh with customers. During a layover in Chicago the two caught a bite to eat in an airport restaurant. Wanting to get better acquainted with their new boss, the employee asked one of those really good icebreaker questions: "So, boss, if you could be any superhero, who would you want to be and why?" Without the slightest pause the boss replied, "Commissioner Gordon." Puzzled by the boss's response, the employee asked cautiously, "Why's that?" The boss looked up, glared at the employee, and said, "Because Batman did all the work and Gordon got all the credit." For the next 3 years the employee and their teammates experienced the Gordon-Batman paradox nearly every day as their boss took credit for much of the teams' accomplishments.

"Mine, Mine, Mine....No Yours" *(just close enough)*

After a large reorganization,[14] a senior executive was given oversight of a function for which she had little knowledge and even less interest. The added

---

[14] Over the years I have experienced and even initiated several reorganizations, both large and small. I've been fascinated with the illusion leaders have (myself included) that a myriad of operational issues can be resolved with a well-reasoned organizational change. The saying is true: Pick your structure, Pick your problem.

responsibility, though, came with a nice bump in pay, and that was of great interest to the executive. Within days of the reorganization the CEO asked the executive to have her newly assigned function run a detailed analysis on purple-widget production. Not wanting to display her lack of knowledge about purple widgets, the executive acknowledged the CEO's request and set out to make it happen.

The executive summoned Jim, the purple widget team leader, to her office. Peering over her desk she relayed the CEO's request. Jim moved to the edge of his seat and raised several qualifying questions: "What time period does the CEO want tracked, and what regions should we include?" There was silence from the exec as she realized she hadn't thought to ask the CEO those questions. Observing the bewildered look from his boss, Jim innocently offered a helpful thought, "You know, we often get this request from the CEO. Generally, there is an underlying question that can be answered without running production reports." More silence filled the room. Trying to help out his new boss, Jim extended what he considered to be a gracious offer: "If you'd like I can circle back with the CEO to better understand what's driving their question."

Unknowingly, Jim's had tripped a "challenge–response" from the executive, and she quickly shut him down. "That's not necessary," she barked coldly. "I know what the CEO is looking for." Then, with confidence well beyond her knowledge, the executive added the needed clarity: "Pull production for the last 3 years and for all regions." And then, to add greater emphasis, the exec piled on one more detail: "And I need this within 2 days." "You've got to be kidding!" Jim replied. "It will take at least a week to pull this together." "Well that's too bad," the exec said, swinging her chair around to face her computer. "Because you only have 2 days."

In the end, the purple-widget team spent significant overtime producing the reports—reports that were unnecessary and didn't get to the CEO's real questions. When the CEO expressed disappointment with the reports, the executive deflected the criticism to the purple-widget team leader. "Well Jim simply went off and ran these reports." "Really!" the CEO replied with amazement. "I thought Jim would have circled back with me to get more clarity on what I needed!"

This is a classic asshole-boss move. Staying close enough to the effort to be associated with leading effectively when all goes well—but far enough away that if the results are less than favorable, the asshole boss can blame others.

When the asinine behavior first emerges, the team is often caught off guard, and the typical response from the team is, "Wait, what just happened?" As the asshole's behavior continues and intensifies the team begins to realize there is a very serious problem emerging. If there are team members who have experienced ARSe in previous environments, the team's mood can quickly move from concern to panic.

However, if the boss is a known quantity—someone with a reputation in the company as an asshat—the team will typically jump to a mind-set of "everyone for themselves."

Phase 2: The Rebellion and The Empire Strikes Back

As news of the boss's toxic behavior circulates within the team, the fight response kicks in and there's an initial *"Oh no they didn't"* reaction, accompanied with a valiant attempt to push back. This push back is the first branch of a decision tree when our brain conducts a threat assessment. We call this the *fight response,* and it's triggered when we believe we can handle the situation. As we ready for action, adrenaline pours into our bloodstream, the stress hormone cortisol is released, and our metabolism is ready to take on the fight.

Following is one of my favorite "rebellion" stories.

Power to the People
Within the rank and file of a fortune 100 Company a small but nimble group of technology folks emerged who had earned the reputation for quickly

implementing practical solutions to operational efficiency issues. Over time the group was given the nickname "little t", distinguishing them from Corporate IT. As the reputation of "little t" grew they visible on the Corporate IT's radar, and soon "little t" was absorbed into Corporate IT.

The Corporate IT leader in charge of taking on the small technology team was less interested in uncovering best practices for rapid delivery of technology and more interested in keeping things exactly as they'd always been. Ideas coming from "little t" were readily dismissed by the Corporate IT leader, and the members of the group were publicly criticized for their "unsophisticated" approach.

A few months after the integration, the Corporate IT leader was assigned a critical initiative for the company. Initial project estimates from Corporate IT suggested the design phase would take 3 months with another 6 to 8 months for development, test, and delivery. Embedded in the Corporate IT schedule were the seeds of a rebellion.

The small tech team wanted to showcase how their approach could help get to production faster. So at the end of each design session the team would stay after work, building and fine-tuning a proof-of-concept model. Then 2 months into the 3, month design effort the team rolled out a functioning prototype. The customers were amazed to be able to put their hands on a working model of the end product. The prototype greatly aided in finalizing design specs, and it served as the framework for the final product. In the end, the product was delivered 5 months ahead of schedule.

If Hollywood wanted to make a movie about how the underdog saves the day, this would be a great story to tell—were it not for one postscript: The rebellion was forcefully crushed. No matter the fanfare that might surface with a rebellion's minor victory, eventually the asshole boss will exert their dominance, often in a very public way. As Paul Harvey was known to say, "And now, the rest of the story."

Resistance is Futile

On the surface, the small technology team had made a notable contribution to the project. The work product came in ahead of schedule with high quality. Customers were pleased, and the village rejoiced. The "little t" team, however, failed to anticipate the backlash that would come from their new Corporate IT boss, who saw their effort as arrogant grandstanding that undermined the boss's authority. After the glow had faded from the project, the boss made sure the team was uninvited to all key planning meetings and was assigned the least significant projects. Eventually, the team was disbanded and members either left the company or were absorbed into other groups.

The thoughtless and uncaring treatment of the team sent a clear message to the entire Corporate IT group: "Get on the boss's bad side and kiss your career goodbye." Thus, no further rebellions occurred. Coincidently, the Corporate IT team never improved its lack-luster performance.

When I share these stories, the question that often comes up is, "How can a boss get away with leading so poorly? Surely a company would not put up with this." Here is the plain, sad truth. Either a-holes know how to act like jerks and not get fired or the value the jerk delivers is such that organizations disregard their behavior. Occasionally, an ass-clown will cross the line to the point of no return, but for the most part the wheels of asinine behavior continue unchallenged.

Phase 3: Circle the Wagons and Screw the Wagons

In the early reign of an a-hole boss the team will initially attempt to circle the wagons, lock arms and try to fend off attacks. Much of this occurs as bitching sessions and "after" meetings. Stories are widely circulated retelling the latest asshole move, typically in a "he said/she said" genre. There may be discussions about formalizing a counteroffensive, perhaps going as a team to HR; but this is just talk. For the most part, circling the wagons serves only as a momentary catharsis from the ARSe being endured by the team.

This is because as the reign of a toxic boss continues, the catharsis and perceived security found in a circle of wagons diminishes. Over time the a-hole wears down the team and the bonds of unity dissolve into a mentality in which each person looks out or him- or herself. At this stage, team members may not intentionally sell out their peers but neither will they come to their aid. If someone has to be offered up as a sacrificial lamb, team members readily give up their coworkers——just as long as they themselves are safe. You can almost hear from the rank and file a shout, "Screw the wagons. Its foxhole time!" At this stage people look for any safe haven they can find. When the asshole walks the halls, people scatter. If there are ways to opt out of meetings with the a-hole, people take the out. Self-preservation and the fog of war gives way to the rise of both collaborators and sympathizers.

Phase 4: The Fog of War

At the height of the asshole's reign the impact of ARSe is such that in order to survive sympathizers and collaborators will eventually emerge from their foxholes. Collaborators have many names: "sellouts," "butt kissers," "brownnosers." Collaborators are those who "go along, to get along." They find it easier to make a deal with the devil than to hang on for relief that may never arrive. Deep down inside they've replaced the stress of dealing with an asshole with the tension of suspending their personal integrity for the sake of détente. The apparent ease with which collaborators switch sides makes one wonder: "Did they ever have convictions worth defending?" One thing is certain about collaborators——they will always be on the winning side. Not necessarily the right side, just the winning side.

Standing with the collaborators are the sympathizers. These are the folks who've seen the light and lifted the banner: "If you can't beat 'em, join 'em." Sympathizers are not simply accommodating the asshole. They are, in fact, buying into the notion that to advance and get ahead, you really do have to be an

Sympathizers are the first to exit the organization when the bad boss leaves.

asshole. To this end, sympathizers begin to take on the asshole persona. They become a selfish, mean-spirited, hateful replica of the original. Depending on how long the reign of the jerk endures, sympathizers will get the best promotions and job assignments, burning bridges along the way. While it may be hard to distinguish the sympathizers in the fog of war, they are easily spotted when the asshole leaves. Sympathizers are the first to exit the organization when the bad boss leaves.

CAUTION: In the fog of war, sympathizers and collaborators do not change uniform, so you can tell what side they are on. Unfortunately, you'll not know what side a person is on until it's too late and they've hung you out to dry.

Phase 5: Zombie Land—Dealing with Broken Pieces (People)

If the reign of an asshole is long enough or intense enough for a team to reach phase 4, the damage to trust and unity is nearly impossible to repair. A very good friend of mine personally lived through such an experience. She took over a team that had been so badly mistreated for so long that they were incapable of trusting anyone or anything. The team had endured years of one terrible boss after another, each worse than the last. Over time, honest criticism devolved into contempt to the point that team members could hardly stand working together. My friend tried everything she knew to bring the team out of the fog, to make amends, forgive, and start anew. She'd have moments of hope, brief periods of success when she thought her team was turning the corner, but then someone said or did something that was misconstrued, and old fears resurfaced and the team would fall back into dysfunction. There was no way this group of people would ever be a team. At best they were a workgroup of folks who occasionally collaborated, but only when it was absolutely necessary.

Sadly, it wasn't until most of the folks moved on and were replaced with new team members that the team itself began to heal. Although I understood from a behavioral view how the nature of ARSe was influencing my friend's team, the impact on her, personally, was profound. In the words of my friend, "The experience was one of the saddest and most disappointing of my career."

THE IMPACT AN A-HOLE COWORKER HAS ON PERFORMANCE

You may be one of those fortunate few who've never encountered a really bad boss. Odds are, however, you've encountered a coworker or teammate who just has a knack for making everyone miserable. According to 20 years of research by Georgetown professor Christine Porath, 98% of workers have experienced outright nastiness, intentional undermining or downright uncivil behavior by a coworker. This aligns with research cited by Drs. Twenge and Campbell, noting persistent and widespread reports of abuse and hostility from coworkers. While there may be moments of relief from a really bad boss, toxic coworkers are in your face throughout the day. Getting work done can be difficult enough without the added frustration from a coworker who is acting really badly. To emphasize the point, consider the impact to a team's productivity that surface from a toxic coworker:

- 48% decreased their work effort
- 47% decreased their time at work
- 38% decreased their work quality
- 66% said their performance declined
- 63% lost time avoiding the offender
- 78% said their commitment to the organization declined

The coworker who acts badly exhibits the same distinct character traits of asshole bosses: narcissism, Machiavellianism, and psychopathy. Below are the types of toxic coworkers that I have encountered most often.

The Entitled/The Slacker

These are the coworkers who believe the world owes them a living. "Not fair" is their favorite slogan. If a colleague achieves recognition or advancement due to hard work and achieving results, the entitled coworker complains that "the system is rigged." Their narcissism drives "ruthless selfishness," as Richard Dawkins would say. Perhaps Dawkins had "the entitled" in mind when he suggested that any system that promotes concern for or devotion to the welfare of others "is inherently unstable, because it is open to abuse by selfish others, ready to exploit it." It would be an amazing exercise to review the HR policy manual and note how many guidelines are in place to counteract the actions of "the entitled."

The narcissism of "the entitled" creates a belief that "less work for more pay" is not only possible, but acceptable. As a result, "the entitled" have no compunction about taking more than they deserve, regardless of the impact on their coworkers. In one study involving college students, a bucket filled with candy was passed around. The label on the bucket read "Child Development Lab." Participants were informed they could take as much candy from the bucket as they felt they deserved. Students with the highest proclivity towards an "entitlement" mind-set took the most candy, seemingly unconcerned about, or with a disregard for, the amount of candy remaining for the children.

Slackers have a gift for doing the least amount of work possible. If there is a team project, they contribute little or no effort. What makes slackers persistent asshats is their ability to take credit for others' work, or to blame their poor performance on issues with other people. Slackers survive by the Machiavellian adage that suggests "credit can be easily gained by influence and deception." Slackers, however, tend to miss the second part of the Machiavellian view: "However, credit gained by influence and deception can seldom be retained because of a lack of knowledge or resources."

Drama Kings/Queens

These are folks whose narcissism is fueled by the need to draw attention to themselves. Every event, every encounter is overblown. Hyperbole is their foil, and embellishment is their shield. "This is the person whose workload is bigger than anyone else's, who has the worst flu symptoms during cold season, and whose clients are the most annoying. They thrive on chaos and will one-up any story you have."

A large part of their drama is driven by a deep seated mistrust of almost everyone, nearly leading to paranoia. They have many acquaintances but few friends—because they simply cannot be vulnerable enough to let someone get close enough to hurt them. In the end they see the worst motive or devious intent in the words and actions of others. This mistrust feeds an uncontrollable behavior to spread rumor and gossip, which is supercharged by making worst case assessments from the most mundane and innocent interaction. They look for the worst in people, and they easily find it.

The Intimidator/Bully

Unfortunately, every organization, group, or team finds itself dealing with the occasional bully. Unlike the slacker or drama king/queen, who may go unnoticed for a time, bullies by their very nature stand out. A bully is that person who willfully and maliciously intimidates those around them in order to satisfy their own selfish needs or ambitions.

A Google Trends search on the term *bullying* reflects a steady rise over the past several years. Spikes in the trend line draw attention to alarming facts: Within a 6-month period in 2011 more than 6 million schoolchildren experienced bullying. This intimidating behavior occurs in the workplace as well as the schoolyard.

Behaviors associated with a bully can be related to what is clinically defined as "antisocial personality disorder"—or more colloquially psychopathy or sociopathy. These behaviors include:

- Inability to conform to social norms of behavior (i.e., incivility)

- Deceitfulness and manipulating others for profit or pleasure
- Physical and verbal aggressiveness
- Disregard for safety of self and others
- No remorse (and perhaps enjoyment) for the pain and injury they inflict on others

The little bit of good news is that many organizations have taken a stronger stance in dealing with workplace bullying.

Too Important for a Footnote: A Hostile Work Environment

There is a world of difference between dealing with someone who is an asshole and someone who is intimidating or threatening. I cannot emphasize it enough: If for any reason your interaction with someone at work makes you feel unsafe or at risk, speak up immediately!

If the person of concern isn't your boss, then let your boss know what's going on. Ask that your concern be presented to HR, and request a formal response to your concern. If the person of concern is your boss, go directly to HR.

While I can't speak for every HR function, I can tell you that once HR has been informed of a complaint about a hostile workplace, the organization itself is liable if the concern is not appropriately addressed.

As someone who has headed HR for a number of years, I've encountered occasions when an employee believes HR can't or won't do anything about a complaint of a hostile work environment.

While I can't speak for every HR function, I can tell you that once HR has been informed of complaint about a hostile workplace, the organization itself is liable if the concern is not appropriately addressed. The HR professionals I know and work alongside take such complaints very seriously.

For more information see http://www.eeoc.gov/laws/types/harassment.cfm

The Power Tripper

Power Trippers come in three types: (a) get-ahead-at-all-cost, (b) run-of-the-mill glory hog, and (c) the introverted narcissist. The people in the get-ahead-at-all-cost group, easiest to spot and avoid, are those folks who are on a rocket ship to the top and heaven help the poor soul who gets in their way. They work every angle and seize every opportunity to get ahead. They have a maniacal focus on their career success. Their demeanor is such that they are never happy, never content. Even when they achieve what, for many, would be a pinnacle of success, they want more: more status, money, possessions. Their road to success is paved with broken relationships and sworn enemies. If not for their blatant arrogance, you might have a degree of pity for them.

While the aspirations of the run-of-mill glory hog are a bit less aggressive, they are just as cunning and manipulative in making plays to advance their own gains. Glory hogs are so difficult to work with because you can never be completely sure of their motives. Sometimes they genuinely advance the "greater good." More often, though, they have a hidden agenda focused on promoting their own self-interests. You want to keep these folks at arm's length, and by all means don't turn your back on them. To call them an enemy would be too harsh. To call them a friend would be too much. At best they are a workplace acquaintance.

The last group of power trippers is the introverted narcissists. These folks have typical narcissistic tendencies but without the bravado. They seem to have an insatiable need for validation and affirmation. To be fair, we all need validation and affirmation. Although, at times, our need for validation is even stronger than our need for romantic/emotional connections, for introverted narcissists, the unmet need for validation drives unhealthy workplace behaviors, behaviors often targeted at perceived rivals. This can include actions such as leaving others off important e-mails or not inviting perceived rivals to critical meetings. They want to be included in the important projects but will seldom consider including a rival in a notable effort.

They rarely share credit, while at the same time they can't stand to be "out of the loop." Introverted narcissists are quiet asshats, but they are in fact, nice "enough." Nice enough to be acceptable, even helpful for short periods of time. But their demands for attention and constant grousing and complaining are so exhausting, few people can tolerate them for any length of time.

In the end, power trippers will bemoan any perceived lack of loyalty but will rarely reciprocate loyalty towards others.

Chapter 7: Combating the ARSe Virus

ARSe is an infectious virus! Fighting an infectious disease is very complicated because you must fight the battle on two fronts. On one, you're seeking to reduce and prevent the spread of the infection. On the other, you're monitoring symptoms of the disease and administering treatment. In a very real sense the ARSe virus spreads from person to person resulting in fatigue, issues regulating sleep, depression and emotional detachment. So this is a good place to pause and take a closer look at how the ARSe virus impacts the workplace.

Since 2007 the American Psychological Association (APA) has overseen an annual study entitled: *Stress in America*.[15] Outcomes from the APA's research have provided useful insights on the leading sources of stress, associated symptoms, and recommendations for managing stress.[16] Drawing on the APA's research we say there are basically two types of stress: acute and chronic.[17]

Acute stress occurs in the normal interactions; it can be as simple as feeling as if you always get in the slow line at the checkout counter or finding a scratch on your car. While frustrating in the moment, the causes of acute stress are typically short-lived and can be readily managed.

Chronic stress, on the other hand, occurs as a result of a seemingly never-ending barrage of conflict, chaos, and disorder. The continuous nature of it is such that, for some, the way in which they view the world is negatively impacted. In the case of ARSe, those who have endured painful years working with or around a workplace asshole, find themselves unable to envision, much less experience, an asshole-free

---

[15] You'll find a wealth of information and insights on the APA's "Stress in America" study at their website: http://www.apa.org/news/press/releases/stress/index.aspx

[16] America isn't alone in suffering from stress. See the article in the Wall Street Journal entitled, 'Das Burnout': An Epidemic in Germany. http://www.wsj.com/articles/das-burnout-an-epidemic-in-germany-1464023945

[17] The APA also identifies a third type of "episodic stress," which is brought on by those who are highly pessimistic, disordered or simply given to worry

workplace. If their past boss was a flaming asshole, they will carefully look for, and often see, (real or imagined) signs of asinine behavior in the new boss. (See chapter 6, the section entitled "Phase 5: Zombie Land—Dealing with Broken Pieces (People).")

Like other infectious diseases, outbreaks from the ARSe virus can spread rapidly, and containment is problematic. According to the Mayo clinic, infectious diseases are disorders caused by organisms such as bacteria, viruses, or parasites (the last is an apt description of a workplace asshole). Infectious diseases can be spread by insect or animal bites. Many infectious diseases are spread by consuming contaminating food or water. The ARSe virus, however, is spread from person to person, most often by coming into direct contact with "patient zero" (also known as the workplace asshole). ARSe can also be passed "downstream," as those infected come into contact with others in the workplace. Depending on the influence a workplace asshole exerts, an entire eco-system can become contaminated—be it a department, function, or the whole organization. In this condition, many will be infected with ARSe simply by entering the environment.

Fighting the infectious nature of ARSe is complicated because workplace assholes are just carriers of the disease; they are totally immune to the effects of ARSe themselves.[18] From my experience I've seen two effective approaches in dealing with the ARSe virus: (1) treatment and prevention and (2) dealing with workplace assholes.

TREATING ARSE

Let's return once more to the APA's studies on stress and specifically stress management. A search on the APA's website for information on "stress management" returns over 21,000 references—everything from journal articles to book chapters. In fact, there is an entire scientific journal devoted to managing stress that's been in

---

[18] The technical term is asymptomatic carrier: an individual who serves as host for an infectious agent but who does not show any apparent signs of the illness.

publication since 2003.[19] There's also the American Institute of Stress which is committed to "[improving] the health of the community and the world by setting the standard of excellence of stress management in education, research, clinical care and the workplace."[20]

Thankfully (and sadly), there is a wealth of information available on managing stress. The challenge is boiling this information down into simple, practical applications for the treatment and prevention of ARSe.[21] Over the years I've found a two-part treatment protocol to be effective at treating (1) ARSe: taking care of yourself and (2) not forgetting what's important.

Treatment Priority 1: Take Care of Yourself

With this treatment protocol,[22] you pay attention to how you are reacting to ARSe and deal with unhealthy habits. You find time to disconnect and get away; to kiss, cuddle, and hold hands [my favorite]; and find encouragement.

Paying Attention

If you've done any flying you'll remember the safety message where flight attendants warn if there's a loss of cabin pressure, oxygen masks will drop down front of you. Remember the drill? Put your mask on first before you try to help others. The first priority in the treatment of ARSe is to "Take Care of Yourself." This is not to be taken as "Everyone for himself or herself." Rather, to take a moment and make sure that you are doing okay.

---

[19] International Journal of Stress Management: http://www.apa.org/pubs/journals/str/index.aspx

[20] http://www.stress.org/

[21] The approach I've used to craft treatments for ARSe is twofold: (1) Draw on "qualified sources" to find common patterns and themes for stress management, and (2) align these patterns/themes with real-life experiences in which ARSe was successfully treated.

[22] A medical protocol is a detailed plan of treatment or procedure to address an illness or disorder.

"Taking care of yourself" begins with being mindful of how you are doing physically and emotionally. While this sounds easy enough; most people affected by a-holes are so caught up in workplace drama they are unaware of the impact ARSe is having on them. To help gain a better sense of how you're doing, the APA recommends keeping a journal:

> Track your stressors. Keep a journal for a week or two to identify which situations create the most stress and how you respond to them. Record your thoughts, feelings, and information about the environment, including the people and circumstances involved, the physical setting, and how you reacted. Did you raise your voice? Get a snack from the vending machine?

Paying attention to what your body is telling you and how you are reacting to ARSe will help you identify unhealthy habits that may be emerging. For example, issues with eating and sleeping are common ARSe-related symptoms. When people are dealing with stress in general, and ARSe in particular, their eating patterns can be impacted significantly. Personally, during times when I've encountered ARSe, I lose my appetite. Over time, as I continue to go without taking in enough food, my body begins to compensate by conserving energy and I become lethargic and tire easily. This creates an alarming cycle in which I'm not eating because I'm tired, and I'm tired because I'm not eating. Eventually, I have to force myself to eat (to be honest, my wife has to make me eat). The opposite can likewise occur as ARSe compels some to stress eat. There's a reason we label things as *comfort food*. Before too long, overeating related to ARSe has folks digging in the closet for their "big" clothes and dealing with the health issues related to such stress eating.

Problems regulating sleep is another common effect of ARSe. Most often experienced is the inability to get enough sleep; the converse can likewise occur, with some people spending too much time sleeping. At present, the CDC has sounded a national warning about the health and public-safety dangers associated with insufficient sleep. Based on the conversations I hear from my HR colleagues around the U.S., concerns related to sleep disorders will soon become a major issue for health-care providers. Although you could fill several chapters on the topic of sleep, I've found no easy or cure-all answers for ensuring a restful night's sleep other than the common-sense tactics everyone knows: Limit caffeine late in the day, don't have a TV or computer in your bedroom, and avoid stimulating activities before you turn in for the night.

We cannot leave the subject of ARSe and unhealthily habits without addressing concerns relating to substance abuse. This is especially important for those who struggle with addictive behaviors. Consider the following:

Researchers have long recognized the strong correlation between stress and substance abuse, particularly in prompting relapse. Although exposure to stress is a common occurrence for many of us, it is also one of the most powerful triggers for relapse to substance abuse in addicted individuals—even after long periods of abstinence.

Although exposure to stress is a common occurrence for many of us, it is also one of the most powerful triggers for relapse to substance abuse in addicted individuals—even after long periods of abstinence.

If you are dealing with the prolonged impact of ARSe and you know that you struggle with substance abuse, it is important for you to be mindful that there is a high risk of relapse. Ensuring you have a strong accountability partner in your life is an effective deterrent to this risk: someone who will not only help you avoid a relapse but will also be an encourager with your ARSe treatments (see the section on finding encouragement below).

A bit later we will discuss a root cause of ARSe in the workplace: the loss of control and influence. Without question, the sense of a lack of control can be debilitating. An effective countermeasure is to build a few routines into your day. If possible, eat lunch at the same time each day. Carve out a few specific evenings for regular events such as church on Wednesday nights or an exercise class at set times in the week. Make a habit of getting up 30 minutes earlier and setting a routine of reading the paper, meditation, or time with family.

Getting Away/Disconnecting

Likewise, there is great awareness today about the advantage of taking time to disconnect from work, if only for a few days. To help relieve and treat ARSe symptoms, make a focused effort to get away and *unplug*. Downtime is essential because it allows us to step back and catch our breath. However, unplugging from the 24/7 world has become as much a stress-inducing effort as the work demands we seek to escape.

While getting away with someone you are close to is enjoyable, be sure not to overlook the benefits of having time just to yourself. Psychology points to the importance of interpersonal relationships, but times of solitude are necessary if the brain is to function at its best.

Kissing and Cuddling

On the lighter side in the treatment of ARSe are recommendations from the folks at WebMD extolling the health benefits of kissing, cuddling, and holding hands. So that I avoid any criticisms of a hidden motive, here are the facts:

A study of 2,000 couples showed that those who frequently kiss on the spur of the moment are less impacted by stress than couples who only kiss during love-making. According to science, "Kissing relieves stress by creating a sense of connectedness, which releases endorphins, the chemicals that counteract stress and depression."

Researchers likewise found that holding hands and hugging can measurably reduce stress. Fifty couples were asked to hold hands for 10 minutes and then to hug for 20 seconds. A second group of 85 people rested quietly, not touching their significant others. The couples were then asked to talk about a past event that left them angry or anxious. Couples who had not cuddled before revisiting an unpleasant event showed signs of elevated heart rate and blood pressure, but couples who had previously hugged and held hands weren't nearly as ruffled. According to science, "The gentle pressure of a hug can stimulate nerve endings under the skin that send calming messages to the brain and slow the release of cortisol." (see, science says we should cuddle and hold hands).[23]

Find Encouragement

The very best treatment for ARSe is to find a source of encouragement. Let me be really clear here: I'm talking about someone in your life who can and will invest their time and energy to extend you warmth, kindness, and compassion. There is a keen distinction between something that is encouraging and someone who is an encourager. An inspiring movie or song is encouraging. A pet can be encouraging. An encourager, however, is a person who will walk with you through your hardest times. The key in finding encouragement rests in nurturing strong, healthy relationships. This is problematic in itself because most of us have few, if any, really strong, close relationships. Consider these observations:

Decades ago, people typically told pollster's that they had four or five close friends, people to whom they could tell everything. Now the common answer is two or three, and the number of people

---

[23] The science also suggests that a hug from a friend can be helpful in managing stress, but as an HR professional I would offer a word of caution. While a hug from a friend might offer temporary respite, the consequences of hugging someone who doesn't want to be hugged may prove to be more stressful than when you started.

with no confidants has doubled. Thirty-five percent of older adults report being chronically lonely, up from 20% a decade ago.

The whole conviction of my life now rests upon the belief that loneliness, far from being a rare and curious phenomenon, peculiar to myself and to a few other solitary men, is the central and inevitable fact of human existence. (Thomas Wolfe)

Despite the advances of modern science, those living in affluent societies today are more isolated than ever before. This isolation stands in ironic contrast given the apparent connectedness of social networks. Humans are intensely social beings. We live isolated lives because modern technology allows us to. And we are blinded to how these individualized lifestyles are brutalizing our humanity. Where do you go when you need someone to stand beside you? (Sabastian Junger, Tribe)

Finally, the BBC's Loneliness Experiment found that "loneliness is more than being socially isolated—it's about being disconnected from deep and meaningful personal relationships."

The first challenge to finding encouragement is the very, very small group of close relationships we have to draw on. The second challenge is that most of us hesitate to let people know how we are doing. There is a comical montage on YouTube of Joey from *Friends* running his famous line, "How you doin' ?" For fun take a minute sometime and count how many times you ask someone in passing, "How you doing?" or "How's it going?" The sad thing is we really aren't interested in knowing how things are going with others. "How you doing?" has become another way of saying, "Hello." I caught myself saying "How you doing?" to a colleague, and I kept walking by, not even allowing my

Before we can find encouragement, we have to be transparent and vulnerable enough to share how we're doing.

colleague an opportunity to respond to my question. How sad.

It should trouble us that we live in a time where most of us are uninterested in knowing how our friends and colleagues are doing. We should also be concerned that when we are going through hard times, we are reluctant to let anyone know. It's fascinating to observe the difference between men and women on this score. I recall hearing a researcher at CCL note that women often feel they are the only ones who are struggling and generally will not ask for help. Men on the other hand know that other men have the same struggles; they just don't want to talk about it. Before we can find encouragement, we have to be transparent and vulnerable enough to share how we're doing.

To understand why encouragement is one of the best treatments for ARSe you really need to appreciate the isolation and fear associated with the virus. The best visual I've found to describe the emotional impact of dealing with workplace assholes is the experience of white-water-rafting.

ARSe is like being in the middle of a raging river—not on the river paddling a raft as it bounces along fast-moving water, but in the white water as you're tossed from the raft into foam and turmoil. If you've ever found yourself suddenly in the middle of a fast-moving river, you know the feeling of helplessness and fear. The panic that hits can be paralyzing as you look for anything that will help you keep your head above water. If you can, you'll reach out and hang on to a boulder, even though the water tries to both squash you and peel you from the rock. As you hang on for life itself, the only questions are, "How am I going to get out of this mess?" and "Will anybody help me?" Using this visual has helped me reflect on the three types of people you'll encounter when you're suffering from ARSe.

The first person is someone who has sympathy for your troubles, but they are too far removed to be of any real help. They see that you're in trouble and feel bad for you. They offer kind thoughts such as, "Don't let go of that rock," and they even give heartfelt prayers such as, "God please help that man." Their concerns don't bring about tangible aid, though. It's not that they don't want to do more; it's just that they are not able to do so, either because they lack the insight on what to do or don't have the resources needed to do more. These folks are most characterized by the "recency effect." When they are near the person facing a hardship, their sympathy is quite visible. The farther away they are from the person in need, either in time (the duration of the trial) or distance (physical separation from the trial), the less connected they are for the person in need. This is not a criticism, just an observation.

The second person you'll meet when you're in the ARSe river is someone who will come along side you and use whatever resources they have available to support you, lift you up, and help get you back on your feet. They are "doers," and they have the will and means to help. They'll throw you a line, make a call, whatever they can. They are like sand on an icy road; they help give you traction. They may have an affinity with the condition being experienced, such as a cancer survivor readily connecting with someone who has just received a disturbing report from their doctor. The gift of encouragement is at work within this person. They are moved beyond sympathy (feeling), towards empathy (action).

The last person you'll meet is someone whose care and concern are such that they will get right into the river with you. They can't simply sit on the shore or offer whatever resources they have available. This person will jump into the river and ride the waves with you. They are usually your spouse, family, or the very dearest of friends. They are the ones whose heart breaks with yours, whose tears and prayers reflect tenderness and grace. It's been said that "there is no hurt like the hurt that comes when someone you love is in pain." Parents know this all too well for "there is no more fervent a prayer than that of a parent for a child."[24] To which I would add, "and

> **The last person you'll meet is someone whose care and concern are such that they will get right into the river with you.**

24 Matthew Henry

the prayer of a spouse whose loved one is deployed during times of war."[25]

This brings up an interesting topic about encouragement: If you're married or in a serious relationship and suffering from ARSe, "Do you tell your spouse/partner?" In the years I've worked with people dealing with workplace assholes, I've seen two sides of this question. Some people share that the support and encouragement they received from their spouse/partner provided the needed strength to get through a very difficult time. Others have expressed deep reservations about discussing how bad things were at work with their spouse/partner because they didn't want to unload their burdens on someone they deeply love. Another reason for avoiding sharing with a spouse is a belief that their mate would not understand or relate to their workplace complexities, much less be supportive for the burden they carried.

There was a time when I would counsel one approach as better than the other. Over time, as I've observed people dealing with and recovering from ARSe, I've come to see both sides. Some people find great support and encouragement in talking with their spouses. Others who attempt to share their burdens with their spouse, instead of encouragement, found criticism for being weak and letting someone walk all over them. In one couple, ARSe nearly destroyed their marriage. In the end, whether to seek encouragement from one's spouse or partner is a very personal decision.

At this point I must to offer a word of caution:

If you opt not to seek encouragement from your spouse, you will eventually need to find someone who will stand with you through this difficult time. Whatever you do, avoid at all costs drawing on someone for encouragement who is of the opposite sex and who you

---

[25] My dad was a sergeant in the U.S. Army. He deployed twice to Vietnam. One of my earliest memories is my mom bringing all the kids together at bedtime and hearing her prayers for dad's safe return.

might find an attraction toward. Dealing with ARSe is a very personal experience and it will leave you vulnerable and exposed. What might begin as a kindness from someone to help you through a difficult time, may evolve into something more. And in the end your stress and condition may become much, much worse than simply dealing with a workplace asshole.

I will also add this note to encouragers:

If you are someone who is providing encouragement to a friend dealing with ARSe, there are a few thoughts to consider. First, try and put yourself in their shoes. Imagine what it would be like if every day you gave your very best at work, only to be met with apathy or hostility; that no matter what you did, it's not good enough, taken for granted, or not credited to you. Imagine the hole in your life from getting nothing in return for all your effort. Making a connection to the trial an ARSe sufferer is enduring will help tune your empathy and allow you to provide greater support. In *Just Listen,* Mark Goulston highlights this point when he notes how we feel such a release when someone acknowledges our pain or our triumphs. Leveraging Goulston's work we find an area where encouragers can be of great help to those dealing with ARSe: listening.

Listening is one of the most selfless and difficult skills to master because you suspend your own ingrained needs for attention and validation in favor of someone else's needs.

Listening is not waiting to talk! Listening is not waiting to talk! Listening is about being totally interested in what someone is saying. When someone is going through a difficult time in their life, taking time to simply listen shows that you care.

To be effective in your listening it can be helpful to understand how people process emotions. To this end, Goulston outlines the typical steps people will go though as they deal with difficult issues. Step 1: I'm screwed and there's nothing I can do about it. Step 2: I'm stuck—this is a big pile of crap and I just have to deal with it. Step 3: This stinks, but I do have options. Step 4: Remember what's important and refocus priorities. Step 5: Build and work a plan to deal with difficult circumstances.

Finally, here are some very helpful insights and tips from Goulston on how to listen:
- Listening allows people to put into words how they are feeling. When people verbalize their hurts and emotions it allows them to "un-jack" their brains.
- When people are venting, don't interrupt, especially to judge or criticize what they're saying—even if what they are saying doesn't make sense. Let them talk as long as they want.
- Sometimes, after venting for a while, a person will pause out of exhaustion. Don't confuse this pause as your invitation to start talking. Be silent and let them catch their breath. One tip that may be helpful is to say, "So, tell me more…" and see what comes next.
- Be guarded against offering "quick-fix" advice. Just listen!

A final word on listening: When you're listening to someone share how they are doing in dealing with a workplace asshat, don't be quick to chime in with your two cents. Keep in mind the acronym WAIT: Why Am I Talking? When we are in casual conversations we often look for opportunities to add our own thoughts: holding up our end of the conversation. To be honest, we want to be seen as having something of interest to share. When you are listening to someone in pain, it's more important to be *interested in the person sharing* than to share something *interesting* in the conversation.

Treatment Priority 2: Don't Forget What's Important

With this treatment protocol you Keep top-of-mind the things that really matter, make tangible progress towards long-term goals, and be clear on how much is enough.

What's Really Important?

"The secret to life is one thing...Find that out, and nothing else matters." (Curly's Law from the movie *City Slickers*.)

In 2002 Rick Warren wrote *The Purpose Driven Life* to help readers consider the most basic and fundamental of questions we all have: "Why am I here?" and "What is the purpose of life?" Warren clearly touched on a need as his book has become one of the bestselling non-fiction titles of all time (32 million copies and growing). The power in Warren's work is that he helps us all refocus our attention on the things that really matter.

I have a friend who suffered a severe heart attack a few years back. Thankfully he recovered. He shared that while he was in the hospital wondering if he would ever walk out, he thought a lot about what he'd done in life and what he still hoped he'd be able to do. Lying in his hospital bed he never once wished he'd spent more time at work, made one more meeting, or tackled one more major project. His most poignant sentiment, that stays with me even to this day, was this: "When you're not sure you will see tomorrow, all that matters is who you love and who loves you."

Work is important. And for men in particular a great deal of our self-worth is found in our work.[26] There is a lie that organizations tell employees that goes something like this: "Who you are is not what you do." This is absolutely not true, even though this saying is often bandied about when reductions in force occur (RIFs, layoffs, and so on). The truth is, there is nothing better than to have a job you really enjoy.[27] This is because, as Rick Warren would say, "It's not about you." Meaningful work affords us the opportunity to be connected to

---

[26] While women, also find a high degree of self-worth in their careers, they are on the whole, much more balanced, drawing equal meaning from work, family, and community. Men on the other hand will often sacrifice important parts of their lives to give more energy to their careers. The HR word used to describe this is "immersion".

[27] Check out the book of Ecclesiastes chapters 2, 3, and 5.

something bigger than who we are individually, which is a need within all of us, even at a young age.

I have a good friend who served as executive director with Youth for Christ. YFC is a faith-based organization that works with middle and senior high school students. According to my friend, kids are driven to be involved in something that makes a difference. They yearn to be a part of something that's important: bigger than them. Fascinating. It would seem that what middle and high school kids are seeking is exactly what we are all looking for.

A key in treating ARSe is to keep in mind what is really important. I appreciate Greg McKeown's book *Essentialism* for helping me reflect on my priorities. I have a bias for taking action, even when I'm not completely clear on a detailed plan of action. I believe this tendency emerges as a passive-aggressive response to how I experience the glacial speed at which most organizations move. Rather than making decisions reactively, I do much better when I distinguish the urgent from the important. To this point, McKeown offers some helpful tips:

- Only a few things really matter, so make it a point to know what those few things are.
- Every decision is a set of trade-offs, so understand what's gained and what's lost.
- Slow down; take the time you need to make clear, well-reasoned decisions.
- Every event holds a lesson, even the events that really suck.

The Long-Game

Another factor in treating ARSs is to keep the long game in mind. We can endure long periods of difficult times if we can see or anticipate an end or a goal. For example, athletes can push their minds and bodies in extreme conditions, knowing there is finish line to cross or a goal to achieve. Consider the story of Florence Chadwick, who in 1952 sought to be the first woman to swim from Catalina Island to Palos Verde on the California coast (26 miles).

The weather that day was challenging because the ocean was ice-cold, and the fog was so thick she could barely see the support boats that followed her. The tides and current were against her. And, to make matters worse, sharks were in the area. But at daybreak she decided to go forward anyway, expecting the fog to lift in time.

Hour after hour she swam. The fog never lifted. Her mother and trainer followed her in one of the support boats encouraging her to keep going. While Americans watched on television other members of her support crew fired rifles at the sharks to drive them away. She kept going and going. At about the 15 hour point she began to doubt her ability to finish the swim. She told her mother she didn't think she could make it.

Unfortunately, at 15 hours and 55 minutes she had to stop and with huge disappointment she asked her support crew to take her out of the water. Because of the fog, she could not see the coastline so she had no idea where she was. She soon found out, however, that she was less than a mile from the coast. She could have certainly reached it if she had just stayed in the water a few minutes longer.

Later she told a reporter, "Look, I'm not excusing myself, but if I could have seen land I know I could have made it." The fog had made her unable to see her goal and it felt to her like she was getting nowhere. Two months later she tried again. And, though the fog was just as dense, this time she kept going. Her time was 13 hours and 47 minutes breaking a 27-year-old record by more than two hours and becoming the first woman ever to complete the swim.[28]

---

[28] http://www.huffingtonpost.com/don-meyer-phd/so-near-and-yet-so-far_b_3714989.html

Recall that the key causes of ARSe are the unrelenting demands, demeaning behavior, disrespect, and general disregard for common workplace civility, all of which continue for seemingly interminable periods of time. Not knowing when, or even if, things will get better places unimaginable stress on a person. Setting milestones towards a long-term goal can help the ARSe sufferer cope with uncertainty. Keeping the long game in mind should not be used to endlessly endure an intolerable situation. Setting milestones, however, can help manage your recovery from ARSe. For example, you can set a goal to hit a certain tenure milestone, build a specific equity position, or realize a defined bonus payout cycle. Keeping the long game in mind can establish a limit you can manage toward; it gives you line of sight to the shore.

> **Keeping the long game in mind can establish a limit you can manage toward; it gives you line of sight to the shore.**

That said, I can speak from my own personal experience with ARSe that sometimes even seeing a shoreline isn't enough to stay in shark-infested waters. I walked away from a job I really enjoyed with a company that was fantastic because I had two bosses that were flaming assholes. Even the golden handcuffs weren't enough enticement to keep me in that arduous situation. Even so, things do seem to work out in the end. The saying has merit: "Everything will be okay in the end. And if it's not okay, it's not the end."[29]

How Much is Enough?

We all need to guard against the "undisciplined pursuit of more." In *How the Mighty Have Fallen,* Jim Collins points to five stages of decline that occur when successful businesses lose focus and succumb to distractions. One stage Collins identifies is the "undisciplined pursuit of more": aggressively pursuing more wealth, more fame, more power, for no other reason than it can be done. In *Essentialism,* McKeown

---

[29] While this saying is often attributed to John Lennon, it became popular in the movie The Grand Marigold Hotel.

cautions each of us against our own insatiable desire for more. My dad had this saying, "What's the difference between a man with five million dollars and a man with five kids? The man with five million dollars wants more. The man with five kids has had enough."

I was coaching a senior executive who had hit a career wall in the organization. A series of mergers and realignments had resulted in this leader's career hitting a stand-still. The difficult question was, "What's next?" This person was pulling down a seven-figure salary and had a fairly influential position but wanted more. Not more money per se, but more power and influence. Most people in his organization aspired to what the executive found unfulfilling; but to be fair, this is true for all of us. Whatever discontent we find within our current status, there are many others who would gladly exchange places with us. The question we need to ask ourselves is: "How much is enough?" Or more to the point: "What are we pursuing and why?"

PREVENTING ARSE

If you're like most people, every flu season you wrestle with taking the time and effort to get a flu shot. You know it's a good idea, even if this year's shots are for last year's flu strain. "An ounce of prevention," as the saying goes. Yet you never get around to it, even though you're convinced each time you drive by the sign at the pharmacy highlighting the availability of shots. Do you know who rarely misses getting their flu shot? Those who know catching the flu would be very risky to their health—and folks who caught a really bad flu last year.

If you've suffered through ARSe, you know all to well the misery it creates. Those recovering are quick to protect themselves from ever catching the virus again. Sometimes this avoidance is done in a healthful manner; other times the avoidance comes at the high cost of poor or missing relationships.

The Vaccine

Recall that ARSe is not a biological virus that invades our body. It occurs from negative experiences that invade our brains and influence

This "virus of the mind" is often referred to as a meme, a term coined by Richard Dawkins to describe how our ideas/ beliefs imitate cultural norms by jumping from brain to brain, much like a virus.

how we think and act. Yet experiences—or more to the point, ideas, beliefs, and behaviors spread from person to person, from one mind to the next, faster than any virus would spread. This "virus of the mind" is often referred to as a *meme,* a term coined by Richard Dawkins[30] to describe how our ideas/beliefs imitate cultural norms by jumping from brain to brain, much like a virus. We see this when a YouTube clip or a post on Facebook post "goes viral." What makes the ARSe virus so damaging is how the disease tears down a person's sense of self-worth. The constant demands, demeaning behavior, and disrespect, combined with hopelessness for any relief, can drive even those with the strongest resolve to lose heart.

What we need is a vaccine to protect us from the ARSe mind-virus. So how do vaccines work? When our body encounters a virus for the first time, white blood cells are produced to attack and get rid of the infection. Depending on the strength and severity of the virus, the body can take several days to figure out exactly what white blood cells are needed to fend off the infection. In some cases, the virus moves too fast for the body to figure out what to do, and serious medical problems emerge. However, when the body successfully fights the infection, it remembers what it did, and if the virus returns, the body quickly produces the needed white blood cells. Vaccines help the body more quickly figure out what white blood cells are needed to fight a specific virus. This is done by having the vaccine imitate the virus, albeit in a less potent form. Once the imitated virus is defeated, the body remembers how to fight that disease in the future.

---

[30] Because I reference Dawkins a few times in this book, I'm compelled to add a note. I believe Dawkins has made remarkable observations in his attempt to understand and explain human nature. What I do not share are the conclusions he has drawn from these observations.

So how do we create a *mind-vaccine* that can protect us from the ARSe mind-virus? To answer this let's take a brief look at how our brains build and use memories. Whenever we encounter something new, the first question our brains ask is, "Will this kill me?" This threat/response trait goes back to days when humans openly shared living space with animals that wanted to eat us. Those humans who were guarded when seeing a new animal had a better chance of surviving than humans who wanted to pet the cute, fuzzy tiger. Over time, the ability of our brains to discern effective threat/responses has been refined. While we don't consciously ask, "Will this kill me?" we do subconsciously evaluate the potential for harm when we encounter something new. Some have described our brains as an inference engine; when our brains take in new information or encounter a new experience, they seek to infer and categorize the new against what they already know (or think they know). Let me illustrate:

When my granddaughter was 2 years old she encountered her first honey bee. She had seen and experienced butterflies before, so for her the bee didn't register as a threat. Before an adult could shoo the bee away she was stung. Thankfully she's not allergic to bee stings, but the horror was nonetheless traumatic (lots of crying and promises to buy her a car). Later that day, after the tears were long gone, a puffball (the floaty thing that dandelions make) floated in front of my granddaughter. Her brain quickly inferred this was another bee and she began to scream and cry. The mind-virus that my granddaughter's brain created with the bee sting was that anything flying or floating near her was going to be painful. So naturally, these things should be avoided. Now, after a few additional experiences, my granddaughter's brain has created a mind-vaccine that helps her better manage experiences with bees, butterflies, and puffballs.

In my experience working with ARSe sufferers, I've encountered both positive and not-so-positive outcomes from ARSe. The positive outcome occurs when the problem person is not in the picture (either the asshole or the ARSe sufferer left the workplace); and the ARSe sufferer, by using the treatment options outlined above, regained and strengthened their self-confidence. In essence, once their brain dealt with the ARSe mind-virus, new memory paths were established that allowed them to better fend off a future encounter with the ARSe mind-virus.

A not-so-positive outcome occurs when ARSe treatments are ineffective (or applied improperly) and the duration of the workplace a-hole(s) continues interminably. At this point an ARSe sufferer's behavior becomes aberrant, straying from what most of us would define as "normal" workplace interactions. The outcome is an inability to build healthy, trusting relationships and a debilitating paranoia that sees the worst possible outcome or the ugliest intentions in nearly every workplace interaction.

In the most extreme cases of ARSe the effect can be so severe and the stress so intense that it leads a person to believe suicide is their only option. An illustration is helpful. The U.S. Army defines toxic leaders as "leaders who consistently use dysfunctional behaviors to deceive, intimidate, coerce, or unfairly punish others to get what they want for themselves." Private First Class Frank Costabile was someone who experienced first-hand the most severe ARSe impact from toxic leaders. In 2013 he was discharged from the Army after his third threatened/attempted suicide. Listen closely to how Costabile characterizes his experience:

> "I just had feelings, like, that nothing's ever going to change. I'm going to get [expletive] every day, and I just don't want this anymore. And I just felt like I wanted to kill myself."

Research by the Army into the cause and effect of toxic leaders uncovers complicated and tragic observations:

- In addition to major problems in their personal lives, the victims also had a [toxic] leader who made their lives hell.

- Sometimes a couple of [toxic] leaders would take turns seeing who could make a soldier's life the most miserable by dreaming up the worst experience or come up with the worst duties.
- While the evidence did not show toxic leaders were the sole cause leading soldiers to commit suicide, soldiers' friends said that toxic leaders had helped push their friend over the brink.
- According to one researcher involved in the Army's study, "When you're ridden mercilessly, there's just no letup; a lot of folks begin to fold."

So is there a way to create an ARSe vaccine without having to actually endure the trials of working with an asshole? Yes: by giving our brain the experience of working with or for a person who acts badly, but, ideally, in a less threatening/damaging manner. Then, once our brain deals with the ARSe vaccine, new memory paths are established that can better fend off a future encounter with the ARSe mind-virus.

The mechanism we can use for developing an ARSe vaccine is found in the concept of learning agility. Learning agility is the willingness and ability to learn from [past] experiences and subsequently apply that learning to perform successfully under new or first-time conditions.

The beauty of Learning Agility is that the learning experience doesn't need to be first-hand. We can learn from the experiences of others. I saw this directly when I had the honor of watching the 82nd Airborne Division perform a night jump at Fort Bragg. Hundreds of soldiers marched onto waiting aircraft, then jumped, at night onto a field where just minutes before Humvee's and artillery cannons had parachuted and landed. While we were waiting for the planes to circle around to the drop zone, I asked the Army officer guiding my visit a few questions:

Me: "How do you motivate a solider to jump out of a perfectly working plane?"

Army officer: "Soldiers don't need a cheerleader telling them it's important they do a good job. Soldiers want a leader who will jump when they jump. And the base commander is the first out of the plane each time we jump."

Me: "Isn't it dangerous to have the soldiers land in a field where you've just dropped Humvee's and cannons? Do soldiers sometimes land on these?"

Army officer: "Sometimes. But it's much better than having a Humvee or cannon land on a solider." (This ended the debate, "Are there such things silly questions!")

What I found interesting was the training that soldiers received. There were countless hours committed in training soldiers on the right way to land. The most intriguing training, however, was a video that showed what happens when someone doesn't land the right way. Watching the video was really difficult: lots of broken bones, sprains, and worse. The soldiers mind was ingrained with a "vaccine" of sorts that helped them maintain their focus on their training and execute their jumps proficiently.

We can apply this same mind-vaccine by learning from those who have dealt effectively with assholes in the workplace. These folks have an ARSe vaccine working for them. They have the experience, skills, and tools to draw on should they encounter a workplace asshole in the future. The same ARSe vaccine can be transmitted to those who stood beside and supported an ARSe sufferer.

However, ARSe sufferers who were not able to effectively deal with a workplace asshat can find themselves paralyzed should they encounter another asshole in the workplace; or worse, they can see every floating thing that passes by as a bee.

Strengthen Your ARSe Immune System

In my view, affirmation and validation are the most powerful influencers in our lives. We all need validation that what we do has worth and that we are important to someone. An executive once shared with me that while they could easily afford to have someone maintain their lawn, they cut their own grass because it is the one thing they did that they could look over their shoulder and see what they've accomplished.

We all need affirmation, the assurance that we are wanted and cared for. I highly recommend the book *I Loved Jesus in the Night: Teresa of Calcutta—A Secret Revealed.* Mother Teresa noted that the greatest depravity she witnessed was not physical poverty or hunger. It was the anguish of not being wanted, of being forgotten or rejected (the antithesis of affirmation), of having no one. The most tragic of experiences is to die alone.

> Self-centeredness and self-worth share a common thread: "You matter." Although self-centeredness is an inward focus declaring that "I matter to me," self-worth is an outward focus affirming that "I matter to others."

I've noted that the key reason ARSe is so damaging is that it destroys a person's sense of self-worth. In a world that seems to be more and more narcissistic, we need to make a clear distinction between being self-centered and having a sense of self-worth.

Self-centeredness and self-worth share a common thread: "You matter." Although self-centeredness is an inward focus declaring that "I matter to me," self-worth is an outward focus affirming that "I matter to others."

TREATMENT PROTOCOL

In order to prevent the spread of ARSe, you should follow a *protocol* in which you limit exposure, pay attention, and use protection.

Limit Exposure

There's a saying that if you hang around someone who is hot-tempered, over time you'll become hot tempered yourself.[31] We've all experienced this in some fashion. You have a friend who tends to use certain words or gestures. Over time, your brain will begin to mimic these patterns and you'll start using the same words or phrases. The science behind this is fascinating, and we once again go back to meme theory (how our brains imitate the culture around us) for an explanation.

Italian researchers in the mid-1990s were studying brain-wave activity in monkeys as the monkeys ate peanuts. As expected, when they ate a peanut, neurons in specific areas of the brain lit up. During the experiment a monkey happened to see a nearby researcher casually eating some of the peanuts. To everyone's amazement, the same neurons in the monkey's brain fired. Just the act of watching someone eat a peanut created the same neurological response. From this research came our understanding of "mirror neurons": the ability of our brains to "empathically feel" what someone is experiencing, without actually having the experience ourselves.[32]

To help prevent the spread of ARSe, we need to be careful to limit our exposure to workplace assholes. Otherwise, over time we will begin to exhibit the very asinine behavior we can't stand. The sad truth is it's easier to spread "asinine behavior" than the common cold.

Some argue that the best defense against picking up bad behaviors from asshats is to isolate or quarantine them. But that's just

---

[31] Proverbs 22: 24-25 Make no friendship with a man given to anger, nor go with a wrathful man, lest you learn his ways and entangle yourself in a snare.

[32] Recall from Section 1 that individuals with psychopathy fail to make an empathic connection with the feelings of others.

not practical in the workplace, especially if the asshole is your boss. Your best option in dealing with a "bad boss" is to limit your exposure by engaging only in the necessary interactions that allow you to be close enough so that you're not an afterthought and thus stay in the boss's good graces, but don't get so close that the bad behavior rubs off on you.

This is a tricky and delicate balance. Your inclination is to keep your distance and stay off the radar. Believe me when I say, though, that out of sight is not out of mind. Eventually the boss will come looking for you or, even more likely, summon you to their office for an "update." Maintaining some level of ongoing interaction can help make those interactions a bit more tolerable.

Because at some point you'll need to have some level of interaction with workplace assholes, I offer two more suggestions for preventing the spread of ARSe to others: (1) pay attention to your own behaviors and (2) use protection!

Pay Attention

We've discussed earlier the physical and mental impact ARSe suffers encounter. There is one additional consequence of we cannot overlook: the impact on family and friends. Recall that ARSe is spread from person to person. Although contracted most often by coming into direct contact with the workplace asshat, ARSe can also be passed "downstream" as those infected come into contact with others in the home and workplace. Let me offer an illustration of this downstream infection by way of the "Tail-Pinch Experiment."

A senior fellow at the CCL shared with me a fascinating account of a behavioral experiment using monkeys.[33] Monkeys are very social animals, and after being alone for a while, they long for a companion. To observe these behaviors, researchers placed a large red button in the

---

[33] Because humans and monkeys share similar social characteristics, researchers often run behavioral experiments with monkeys in an effort to extrapolate an understanding of human behavior. Sometimes experiences with monkeys are replicated with humans with fascinating similarities (and even more fascinating differences).

monkey cage so that when a monkey became lonely they could push the red button and another monkey would drop into the cage: and voilà–instant companion.

As the experiment continued, the researcher wanted to understand the impact on group interactions when one monkey became upset. So a device was crafted that would allow researchers to sneak up behind a monkey and pinch its tail. Not so hard as to cause harm, just hard enough to really piss off the monkey. During the experiment an unsuspecting monkey was singled out and—ouch—its tail was pinched. The monkey immediately turned and beat the crap out of the nearest (albeit innocent) monkey. The researchers were fascinated with how fast retribution was meted out.

Then a twist was introduced to the experiment. A single monkey was placed in the cage, and when it wasn't looking, its tail was pinched. The monkey began moving erratically around the cage, making lots of noise (undoubtedly monkeys do curse). Suddenly the monkey went over, pushed the red button, and another monkey dropped into the cage. At this point the tail-pinched monkey began to beat the crap out of the new monkey.

When my friend shared this story, I couldn't help but to laugh out loud. Then my colleague shared a key learning from the experiment. When most people hear this story, they end up smiling, laughing, or being annoyed at the mistreatment of monkeys. For those who find a bit of humor in the story, odds are that the humor comes not from the monkey's behavior but because you recognize yourself in the story. If we are honest, at one point or another, we have all been the monkey whose tail was pinched or the monkey who took the brunt of someone else's frustration.

When I told the tail-pinch story to a senior executive at a large pharmaceutical firm, she was nearly speechless; she finally whispered: "That was me, just yesterday." The executive leaned back in her chair and continued, "I had come home from a really bad day at work and my oldest son was lying on the couch watching TV while his coat, shoes, and socks were spread all over the floor. I just unloaded on him! I mean I really got mad and was practically shouting at him to clean up his mess. He got mad right back at me as he picked up his shoes and socks, protesting loudly that the coat was not his. Then he unloaded on his younger brother to get him to pick up his coat. As my younger son begrudgingly stomped into the room to get his coat, he unloaded on our family dog, whose only mistake was sleeping on the chair."

ARSe can have a remarkably harmful impact on how we interrelate with others. Some people react to it by withdrawing. Others lash out. Sometimes ARSe sufferers are erratic in their interactions, becoming not just unpredictable but also impractical. Depending on the influence you have, others you come in contact with can begin to take on the same ARSe symptomology you exhibit. Therefore, it is important that you pay attention to how you are behaving. It is especially important that you have people in your life who will tell you when you are acting badly (perhaps more so than usual).

Use Protection

Unfortunately, there is no such thing as an ARSe prophylactic. There is, however, a way you can protect yourself from the spread of the virus. The roots for this protection are found in Drs. Twenge and Campbell's book *The Narcissism Epidemic*. Noting that in the workplace we are often stuck with the narcissist boss or coworker, the authors suggest the best protection is to put up reasonable boundaries. For example, do not put yourself in a situation where you have to rely on a narcissist's trustworthiness or integrity." In chapter 8 I'll outline how to set boundaries and, when necessary, confront a workplace asshole, whether it's your boss or a coworker. For now, let me make a crucial point. The key to setting boundaries is establishing where the line is long before you get there. It's very easy to fall into an asshat's pattern of behavior without realizing what's happened. For example, a favorite pastime of workplace assholes is to trash talk people behind their backs. Without setting a clear boundary, you can get caught up in these shenanigans in the blink of an eye. Before you know what's happening, you're talking trash about your workplace colleagues as well.

Another form of protection goes back to the suggestion made earlier: Keep a journal of the stress you've endured as a result of the workplace asshole. Making notes of each trying encounter you've had can be helpful in the long run. Speaking as a HR professional, I would say that providing thoughtfully documented details about the behaviors, exchanges, and mistreatments you've experienced while working with a bad actor can be valuable protection should the need arise.

Watch Your Back

In the appendix I outline five levels of workplace assholes. It's logical to think that people at Level 5: (flaming assholes) are the worst of the worst and should be avoided at all costs. In fact, people at Level 4: (sophisticated assholes) are by far the most dangerous type in an organization. This is because they have the strongest disposition towards the psychopath dimension of the Dark Triad behaviors. In a 2004 article, in *Harvard Business Review,* "Executive Psychopaths," Gardiner Morse points out the character traits that make Level 4 assholes so dangerous:

> They're cunning, manipulative, untrustworthy, unethical, parasitic, and utterly remorseless. There's nothing they won't do, and no one they won't exploit, to get what they want. A psychopathic manager with his eye on a colleague's job, for instance, will doctor financial results, plant rumors, turn coworkers against each other, and shift his persona as needed to destroy his target. He'll do it, and his bosses will never know.

Level 4: Sophisticated Asshats are by far the most dangerous people in an organization.

What makes assholes at Level 4 so effective in executing their devious plans is their innate charisma and charm. They are naturally personable, and they put people at ease. Behind this facade is an evil that is only exposed after the trap is sprung. The best defense against a Level 4 asshat is to watch your back. Be mindful for clues such as an overaggressive pursuit to look good, to make their mark, or advance their career. Also, backhanded criticisms or sarcasm about your work or the work of others.

Pay attention to these signs and protect yourself. Most important, be mindful that a sophisticated asshole will look to manipulate and exploit you. They may learn what motivates you and use this to manipulate your efforts. They will seek to uncover and exploit your weaknesses. Again, be on guard and watch your back. Be diligent to keep a journal entry for each time you sense something devious is in play. This may be helpful should your concerns prove valid.

Chapter 8: Dealing with Workplace Assholes

At the risk of overelaborating a point, I want to say again: There is no reason whatsoever anyone should have to tolerate, survive, or endure an asshole in the workplace.

A key goal for this book is to do more than explain why people behave badly, more than make fun of assholes in the workplace. While there is some comfort in knowing that most people encounter such people in the workplace, it doesn't make your situation better. If you're in a situation in which you're confronted with a bad actor, or if someone you deeply care for is contending with an asshat at work, the only question that really matters is, "How do I make this madness stop?" The key in dealing with workplace asshats is realizing something has to change: either with you, with the asshole, or both. In this chapter I'll outline a process for discerning and making the change that is needed: from how to work through the decision-making process, to considering your options to stay or leave.

LESS THAN HELPFUL ADVICE

Often, when you find yourself in real trouble, you get tons of friendly advice that honestly has no practical benefit at all. A pastor friend of mine shared with me that one of the most challenging aspects of counseling was helping those in need dismiss the really bad advice they received from others. His quiet prayer was, "Lord, deliver us from well-meaning but sense-lacking people." Of course, people don't mean to add to someone's trouble when they spout off-the-cuff solutions to extremely hard problems; for instance, when someone says, "Well, just hang in there."

To be clear, there is a difference between surviving and dealing with an asshole. I mentioned earlier the popular book *The No Asshole Rule*, by Ronald Sutton of Harvard University. Dr. Sutton's work has helped frame a healthy conversation about people acting badly at work. However, one aspect of his work that falls short is his advice for surviving nasty people and workplaces. Most of Sutton's suggestions are more about accommodating assholes than actually dealing with them. He acknowledges this point when he writes, "There is a dark side to these ideas. They might provide just enough protection (or, worse yet, fuel enough delusion of protection) to stop people from bailing out of relentlessly demeaning situations—even when they have exit options." In fairness to Dr. Sutton, there is a certain appeal in the straightforwardness of the suggestions he (not to mention others) offers. Yet there are inherent flaws derived from the premise that the best you can do is *survive* a workplace asshole. For example, consider the following less-than-helpful tips: Play and beat the asshole at their game, change how you see things (keep a positive attitude), hope for the best but expect the worst, develop indifference and emotional detachment (ignore it), and fight and win the small battles.

Play and Beat the Asshole at Their Game

Playing the asshole game is akin to swimming with sharks: The only upside is for the shark. The best a-holes are constantly running a mental "upside/downside" calculation in their heads. On every interaction they assess the pros and cons for how they can best leverage a situation to their own advantage. With great practice and dedication, a normal person can learn to play this game. It's very dangerous, though. If you play it long enough you will become the asshole you're fighting. Also, what a normal person has to work at, the a-hole does naturally. No matter how good a normal person becomes at the game, eventually they'll misstep and the game will be over, often with catastrophic results. This deserves an extra warning. Do not be tempted to manage the asshole by playing into their ego, appealing to their vanity in order to gain an advantage. You may think you've built up a few markers you can cash in, but a workplace asshole rarely reciprocates a favor for a favor.

Change How You See Things (Keep a Positive Attitude)

This might be better titled the "rose-colored glasses" plan. Reframing a bad experience so you can gain some learning for future reference is very healthy. For example, taking out the side of the garage because you didn't give yourself enough room is a learning opportunity not to be missed. It stinks, and there is damage that needs to be addressed, but you can learn from it and do better next time.[34]

However, trying to see the "positive" in a continuously toxic work environment ignores the hardships of dealing with a workplace asshole. The motto "Don't worry, be happy" is one of those well-intended, but misguided pieces of advice." Only those who don't live in storm-prone areas of the U.S. would suggest that every tornado has within it the possibility of a visit to Oz.

It is important to acknowledge and own how you're feeling because of the toxic workplace arising from an asshole boss or coworker. I've seen ARSe suffers get to a place where they can move towards a healthy path forward and from these steps begin to find a good and healthy outlook. This came only when a resolution to their misery was established. Whenever I encounter an ARSe suffer who is putting on a brave face, I'm concerned—concerned that just beneath the façade is a heart that is breaking, and repressed emotions that will eventually erupt.

Hope for the Best/Expect the Worse

Hope is not a plan. My daughter is a Marine. When she was on active duty, I paid extra attention to the daily news.[35] One day I saw a reporter interviewing a Marine Major in Iraq whose team had recently returned from a heavy engagement with enemy combatants. As the interview was winding down the reporter asked, "Major, how can you hope to win in this campaign?" The Major quickly replied, "Ma'm,

---

[34] This comes from experience in teaching three teens how to drive.

[35] Which brought back memories of my mom watching the news when my dad was deployed to Vietnam.

hope is not a plan. I can assure you we have a plan and hope plays no part." Then the interviewer asked one final question: "Well, Major, can you tell me if your team won their recent engagement?" An emboldened look came across the major's face as he proudly responded, "Ma'm we're Marines. We always win." At which point a loud "Ooh-rah!" was shouted by those in the background.

Develop Indifference and Emotional Detachment (Ignore It)

Honestly, I can't believe this is even a suggestion. It's like telling someone who works with or for an asshole to be okay with it, find a way to be at peace, and accept that this is just how things are. That is utter nonsense.

Fight and Win the Small Battles

This is akin to the battle cry: "Join the resistance and become a freedom fighter!" Folks may tell stories of your heroics around the water cooler, but this is not a successful long-term plan.

I must confess, I feel a bit like a jerk criticizing well-meaning tips for surviving nasty people and workplaces. In fairness, there are several profound suggestions, such as: "Ask yourself; Are you really trapped." and "Seek support." Exploring these points is where we begin to really figure out how to deal with a workplace asshole.

SOMETHING HAS GOT TO CHANGE

Whether you're working with or for an asshole, and regardless of reasons why people behave the way they do, everything eventually comes down to one simple question: "What can I do about the difficult person I have to contend with at work?" The answer begins with a commitment to making a change in one or all of the following:

The *workplace* has to change (either the asshole leaves the workplace or the workplace motivates the asshole to alter their behavior). Or *you* have to change: (either you change where you work—leave your company or department—or you change how you interact with the asshole).

This type of change doesn't just happen. You need to be intentional on building and working on a plan to deal with a workplace asshat. It does, however, start with acknowledging a change has to be made. For this we can draw on some fundamental concepts as you prepare to build your plan.

Change Versus Uncertainty

Major initiatives for organizational change often result in significant impact on employees. However, long before anything specific is known about the change, the rumor mill kicks in and speculation takes over.[36] A great deal of anxiety surfaces within a workforce when employees get wind of an impending change but haven't been told the details yet. It was during one of these times that an employee shared with me a helpful bit of insight: "Listen, I can deal with change, but uncertainty drives me crazy." Almost everyone in the company knew *something* was coming, but the uncertainty of not knowing what and when was almost unbearable. As nature abhors a vacuum, the brain abhors a mystery.[37]

Recall that our brains are basically an organizing machine. When we encounter a new experience, our brains look to make a connection to a similar experience from our past. When we are overwhelmed with uncertainty, the part of the brain that influences level-headed thinking loses energy to the part of brain that influences instinctive responses. This, in turn, increases our anxiety and tension, which can lead to an inability to think clearly or, worse, make rash, ill-considered decisions.

When you find yourself working with or for an asshole the greatest uncertainly centers on time. How long will I have to endure this

---

[36] I like Mark Twain's saying: "A rumor will be half way around the world before the truth has put on its shoes."

[37] You might hear some folks say they love mysteries. What they really mean to say is they love solving mysteries.

behavior? When will the company wake up and do something? What has to break, or how many customers (or employees) do we have to lose, before a change is made? Most people can endure a hardship, even very severe hardships, if they know there is a fixed duration. My dad did two tours in Vietnam. On both tours the first thing he did was start a calendar to mark off the days until he was able to go home.

The second greatest uncertainty is a deep concern that the workplace a-hole will put your job at risk. If the person is a coworker, you're constantly on guard against being set up to look bad and possibly getting fired. If the asshole is your boss, you fear that they will somehow turn the table, suggest your work is substandard, and send you packing. The uncertainty about how long you'll have to endure a workplace asshole, coupled with the ever-present risk to your job security, serve as a force multiplier that exacerbates ARSe.

ARSe can have a detrimental impact on your decision-making. Make no mistake: The uncertainty in dealing with a workplace asshat can result in a paralyzing effect, a feeling of being stuck with few or no options. As you begin to build your plan to deal with a someone acting badly in the workplace, keep one thought resolutely in your mind: You are not stuck.

Control and Influence

Let's be honest. Most of the major change we encounter in our lives is change that is done *to* us. Occasionally we'll initiate some level of change in our lives—perhaps a new look or a personal commitment to adopt a healthier lifestyle. If we are perfectly honest, though, the big changes we encounter happen because of an external catalyst. For example, significant changes in lifestyle are often preceded by a doctor's report, not internal willpower. It's not surprising when confronting change that we believe we have little control. I was talking with a friend who was relocating because her job was being moved to a different state. "Yeah, I don't want to move, but I have no choice." Of course, that's not true. She did have a choice. The options may not have been attractive, but there were options.

When I counsel people who are in the throes of dealing with a workplace asshole, many feel there is little they can do. They feel absolutely stuck. Again, this is clearly not so. When dealing with such a person we have significant control and influence in areas such as: Where you choose to work; Setting boundaries for behaviors you will not tolerate; How you interact and respond to a workplace asshole.

Control can be defined as how much responsibility you desire and the extent you opt to exert influence in areas such as: decision-making and the actions of others. Control also relates to the responsibility we want or will accept, the degree we want to be seen as decisive and in charge. Consider the following: How much do you want to be in charge/take the lead? How much responsibility do you want to take? How much influence do you want to have?

Loss of control is the wreck we often see at the intersection of personality quirks and external pressures. Consider a scenario that occurs with great regularity between couples. It begins with an innocent question: "What do you want for dinner?" Sometimes in the blink of an eye a simple question leads to a heated argument and cold sandwiches. Why does this happen? Simple: the degree of control and influence wanted and expressed between two people. One person has a need to exert control over the dinner decision. The other person doesn't need to make the decision but would like to have some influence: And that's how the fight started.

PLANNING TO DEAL WITH AN ASS-CLOWN

Here's the bottom line: When you're experiencing ARSe your decision-making ability is greatly impaired. We've heard the **fight-flight-freeze** metaphor that outlines how we respond when we are frightened. Well, the same is true when we are under a great deal of stress; we can become **mindless-muddled-mired**: **mindless** because stress has locked out the part of our brain we use for reasoning; **muddled** because we are overwhelmed with a sense we need to take action *now* and we rely on misguided perceptions; and

mired with a belief there are no good options other than to stay in the miserable situation *or* sacrifice our career just to get the heck out of a toxic workplace.

Before you can realistically assess your options for dealing with a workplace asshole, you have to get in the right frame of mind. We've already outlined two important steps: (1) Find encouragement, and (2) validate what's important. With these two anchors in place, the time is right to engage what I call *plan your plan*. Take time to clear out the clutter, put some of the emotion aside, and pragmatically assess and work through your decision points. The key in breaking free of being mindless-muddled-mired is to, first, unjack your brain, and, second, watch out for false choices; and finally, be realistic in your decision making.

Unjack Your Brain

There's a great quote from the television show M.A.S.H. when Hawkeye is introducing a new doctor (BJ) to the interworking of war-time Korea: "If you can keep your head while all about you are losing theirs, then you probably haven't checked with your answering service."[38] A funny misquote of Kipling to be sure, but there is a compelling question just beneath the surface: "How do you keep your head about you when others are losing theirs?" To answer this question, let me first start by defining (or redefining) the term *brain-jacked*.[39] I use the term to describe what happens when our brains are so overwhelmed we say or do things we later regret.

---

[38] Kipling's poem deserves much better treatment. Here is the first stanza: "If you can keep your head when all about you/ are losing theirs and blaming it on you,/ If you can trust yourself when all men doubt you,/ But make allowance for their doubting too;/ If you can wait and not be tired by waiting,/ Or being lied about, don't deal in lies,/ Or being hated, don't give way to hating,/ And yet don't look too good, nor talk too wise."

[39] Brain-jacked is not a reference to the 2011 syfy novel by Falkner where a 14-year-old boy is caught hacking into a major telecom system and is coerced to work for the U.S. government or go to jail. Nor do I mean brain-jacked to refer to someone who is really smart.

In his book *Mindsight,* Dr. Siegel, clinical professor of psychiatry at UCLA, helps us gain a better understanding of what he calls our seventh sense: the ability to perceive how our minds reflect on various experiences and how this effects our overall well-being. Siegel elaborates:

"Mindsight is a kind of focused attention that allows us to see the internal workings of our own minds. It helps us to be aware of our mental processes without being swept away by them, enables us to get ourselves off the autopilot of ingrained behaviors and habitual responses, and moves us beyond the reactive emotional loops we all have a tendency to get trapped in. It lets us "name and tame" the emotions we are experiencing, rather than being overwhelmed by them."

If mindsight is the ability to step back from how we emotionally respond to an event so we can make clear/rational decisions, then brain jacked is the opposite: being so caught up in the event itself, that you're unable to think clearly and respond rationally. The short-term impact of being brain-jacked is easy enough to spot when you witness someone having a meltdown. The best illustration is when a child pushes just the right button and the parent nearly losses their mind.[40] We've all had the experience of being so upset we lose our mind. The next time this happens, rather than admit you lost your mind, use Dr Siegel's terminology and say you had a "temporary brain dysfunction." It sounds less crazy.

The long-term impact of being brain-jacked is more problematic. Our brains have a remarkable ability to block-out painful experiences so we can temporarily survive or get through a difficult time. If the brain couldn't do this, no woman on the face of the earth would ever have more than one baby.

---

[40] Watch the comedian Sinbad's story about when he talked back to his mom and she lost her mind: https://www.youtube.com/watch?v=GweKDE2Lq8g

When we encounter difficult, painful experiences our brains help us either block out, adapt, or accommodate the pain so we can keep going, and in an immediate sense this may be just fine. In the long term, however, and particularly when the difficult experience is traumatic or long lasting, the adaptation that initially provided the strength to move forward eventually becomes a roadblock to growing and thriving.[41] Here again Siegel offers helpful insight: "When we block out awareness of feelings, they continue to affect us anyway. Research has shown repeatedly that even without conscious awareness, neural input from the internal world of body and emotion influences our reasoning and decision making…In other words, you can run but you can't hide."

The last step in unjacking your brain is to be intentional in distinguishing between how you feel and who you are. We can revisit Dr. Siegel to explain:

Consider the difference between saying "I *am* sad" and "I *feel* sad." Similar as those statements may seem, there is actually a profound difference between them. "I am sad" is kind of a self-definition, and a very limiting one. "I feel sad" suggests the ability to recognize and acknowledge a feeling, without being consumed by it. The focusing skills that are part of mindsight make it possible to see what is inside, to accept it, and in the accepting to let it go, and, finally, to transform it.

It's perfectly fine and understandable to feel sad, frustrated, and angry with having to work with or for an asshole, but who you are is not how you feel. Acknowledge your feelings, but don't allow your feelings to define you. This will lead to a very healthy place: being okay with being in a bad place, if just for a fixed time, but not being okay with tolerating a bad place for an indeterminate time.

---

[41] Consider a person who was deeply hurt from by someone very close. In the short run they may be able to block out the pain to move forward. Yet, if they don't come to terms with their pain, they may struggle to truly and completely trust anyone again.

Beware of False Choices

A weary business traveler arrived at her hotel around 9:30 p.m. after a long day of one flight delay after another. Having missed both lunch and dinner, she was relieved to see the hotel restaurant was still open. Forgoing dropping her luggage in her room, she proceeded directly to an open table. Because it was nearly closing time, she was the only patron in the restaurant as a neatly dressed waiter handed her a menu. "Do you have any specials?" the traveler asked. "Yes, we do. We have a grilled salmon that is served with a choice of vegetables," the waiter replied. "That sounds good. What are your vegetables?" she asked. "Corn," the waiter responded directly. "Well what are my choices?" asked the confused traveler. Matter of factly the waiter replied, "Do you want it or not?"

Over the years, as I have sought to counsel those who are struggling with a workplace asshole, I've been fascinated by how often people feel they only have two options: Either stay and endure a miserable situation or leave and take a pay cut in a lower level job. This is what is referred to as *false choice thinking*. In logic terms, a *false choice* is an approach in which only two extreme options are presented. An example of a false choice might be; "You're either for me or against me." False choice thinking is a common outcome when we believe we're stuck, with little to no control over our circumstances.

In a 2016 *New York Times* interview, Carter Murray, CEO of ad agency Foote, Cone & Belding, was asked to comment on why so many people feel as if they are stuck with a bad boss. Murray's response is noteworthy for anyone suffering ARSe. "Thirty years ago, when people stayed in one company, maybe they felt they didn't have a choice. Today, with the fluidity of the marketplace, you do have that choice. You have a lot more power to understand your options than you did before." [42] As you build your plan for dealing with a workplace asshole, be mindful not to succumb to false choice thinking. To be clear, there is a binary decision that you will need to consider: Do I stay

---

[42] In his early days Murray was so angered by the way his boss treated people that he poured a glass of beer on his boss's head. Personally, I love this story, but I wouldn't recommend it. The story makes for great newsprint but not for a great resume.

or do I leave? Know this however: Staying does not mean enduring or tolerating a terrible work environment. Nor does leaving mean having to take a step down in your career or moving somewhere you'd rather not go.

Be Realistic in Your Decision-Making

"We'd just pulled into the parking lot of our 6-year-old grandson's favorite burger joint when we spotted a sign: "Closed. Out of Business!" Our grandson moaned in anguish, "This is the worst day of my life!" To which I replied, "Be real, son: You're bound to have worse days than this."

Reality Check 1: Will the Workplace Change?

Recall, as ARSe relates to the workplace, there are two areas of change to consider. Either the asshole leaves the workplace or the workplace motivates the asshole to change their behavior. Often, I hear ARSe sufferers asking heartfelt questions such as: How long will the company let this behavior continue? Don't they see how bad things are in the department? Doesn't the company care that customers and suppliers are quitting us?

Here we are faced with the first hard reality: the reluctance of organizations to deal with assholes straight on. This point was emphasized by a 2015 article in *Fortune* suggesting that while only 40% of bosses would get rid of a team member whose toxic behavior was damaging morale, nearly 88% of employees would absolutely take action to remove a workplace a-hole. The fact that most organizations ignore nasty behavior from their employees and leaders is senseless. Assholes create many problems for companies: bad morale, poor workplace performance, and potential legal issues, to name only a few.

Why is this? Why aren't organizations more diligent in weeding out nasty people? Here's my take. Organizations either don't know or don't want to know how bad things are. If they did, well, they'd have to take action. Also, the most important focus of an organization is results. As long as results are being achieved—legally, morally, and ethically—little more matters.[43]

The reluctance to identify and deal with assholes is so bad in some companies that you damn near have to gut a pig in the lobby to get fired. Even then, some companies would simply serve up BBQ. So the number one thing to keep in mind if you work for or with an asshole is to *be realistic* about what organizational change you can expect.

The number one thing to keep in mind if you work for or with an asshole is to be realistic about what organizational change you can expect.

You can gauge the likelihood of a company dealing with nasty employees by observing how directly and effectively the company lives up to what it preaches. Any company worth its salt will have a set of values or principles it purportedly lives by. These are typically found on the company's website or on banners displayed prominently in the corporate office. Just because a company has an admirable set of values, however, doesn't mean it actually lives by those values. As an illustration, here are two values Enron communicated to their employees, customers, and shareholders:

Respect: We treat others as we would like to be treated ourselves. We do not tolerate abusive or disrespectful treatment. Ruthlessness, callousness and arrogance don't belong here.

Integrity: We work with customers and prospects openly, honestly, and sincerely. When we say we will do something, we will do it; when we say we cannot or will not do something, then we won't do it.

To realistically discern if your company will address a workplace a-hole, first ask yourself: Have you seen the company not only define

---

[43] But don't forget: (a) morality is relevant, (b) ethics are situational, (c) clarity regarding legalities is why we have high-priced lawyers.

what behavior a good corporate citizen exhibits but also intentionally set out to hire and develop employees who are aligned towards that definition? The same question is relevant for general workplace behaviors such as respect, integrity, and teamwork. Most importantly, have you seen the company take action with those who lead or behave in contradiction to what the company defines as good and acceptable? If so, then it's possible the company will respond appropriately when made aware of someone behaving badly in the workplace.

If you're still uncertain that your company will take action, then you need to consider the odds, which in my experience goes something like this. For asshole coworkers, the odds are good that the company will take action if there are a number of employees who are also voicing issues, especially if those employees note the behavior of the person is impacting the productivity of others. The odds increase rapidly if the behavior of the co-worker is threatening, abusive, or degrading. The odds are extremely poor if the person is a rainmaker— that is, they produce remarkable results for the company (e.g., an athlete who consistently scores but is a real jerk).

For asshole bosses there is an additional dynamic at play. Again, if the company has a track record of holding leaders accountable for leading well, perhaps the company will take action. By and large, there are two additional factors that will come into play to tip the odds against the company taking action: the leader's level and the leader's tenure. Generally speaking, if the asshole is at the vice president or C-level, the odds that the organization will deal with asinine behavior are low. The same holds true with the leader's tenure. I know this sucks, but it's the way things are.

Reality Check 2: Will the Asshole Change?

The second reality check takes us to this question: "Can an ass-clown change their behavior?" Perhaps there's a better question we need to ask: "Is there a cure for being an asshole?" It seems to me that Goulston may have an angle on a cure when he suggests assholes consider two questions: "Are you an…[asshole] because you enjoy creating misery for others or Are you an…[asshole] because you don't know any other way?" Those who acknowledge the latter have hope. Those who enjoy creating misery for others need clinical help (all kidding aside; they really need to see someone.)

As you begin to build your plan, you have to be careful of becoming overly optimistic that the workplace asshole will change. I've seen a great number of ARSe suffers cling to a hope that a person will see the light and change how they're behaving. They want this so much that they mistake a rare kindness from the a-hole as evidence that change is underway. Sadly, this hope quickly fades with the next insult or demeaning offense. To be fair, there are occasions where a person has an epiphany and genuinely looks to behave better. Although, there are many, many false starts from assholes as well.

For example, if the asshole confides "only" in you that they want to do better and they are committed to improving how they behave, be very suspicious. It may be that they only want *you* to believe they're on the straight-and-narrow path. It's more likely they either want you to back off your criticism or, worse, there's a setup in the works.[44] However, if the person truly has had a "change of heart," you should expect to see some sort of open and frank discussion occur with a broad audience. There may not be a resounding mea culpa, or tears and emotions, but there should be a heartfelt, sincere acknowledgment of poor behavior and a definitive commitment to do better. The icing would be if the asshole asks others to help and hold him or her accountable for better behavior.

Reality Check 3: The Change You Need (and Are Ready) to Make

As it relates to *you*, there are two changes to consider. Either you change where you work (leave your company or department) or you change how you interact with the asshole. This may be the most difficult of reality checks, mainly because most of us stink at honestly assessing how we're doing and our readiness for change. In truth,

---

[44] Just because you're paranoid doesn't mean they're not out to get you.

everyone likes change—as long as someone else is doing the changing (I'm just fine thank you very much; no change needed with me, but you need some work). This may provide insight about the popularity of leadership concepts suggesting it is a waste of time to work on deficiencies in our skills and behaviors and that we are better off to just focus on what comes naturally.[45] The reality is we all struggle to accurately assess how we are doing. In the world of behavioral science this is often referred to as the *Dunning–Kruger effect:* Those who are unskilled in a certain competency or disciple often suffer from an illusion of superiority, rating their own ability as above average, and those highly skilled underrate their abilities, suffering from illusory inferiority.

In order to get our heads wrapped around our readiness for change we must not start with the question, "Do I stay or leave?" Rather, we need to begin with the question, "Am I ready to go or am I ready stay?" Being *ready* to stay or leave is a very different question than *should* you stay or leave. As it relates to your readiness for change, there is an extremely important point to make: In order to deal effectively with someone behaving badly in the workplace, *you* will need to change. You have to and must change. There is no way around this. It's not fair. You did nothing to deserve this, and you shouldn't have to, but regardless if you stay or leave, you will need to change. To make this change, you need to reach down deep and resolve to make those changes that are needed.

There is a common roadblock to assessing your readiness for change that merits a word of caution. Often, I hear those suffering with ARSe say they can't make a change because they are the buffer between the asshole and the team. In many cases this is true, and when a change is made the team is exposed more directly to asinine behavior. However, more times than not, this is exactly what's needed.

---

[45] Books such as "Strength Finders" have gained popularity by encouraging people to focus on what they are good at and ignore weaknesses. Goldsmith's "What Got You Here Won't Get You There" is a strong counter to the "I'm OK—You're OK" philosophy. Also, research by CCL and Korn Ferry provides solid evidence that inattention to weakness will, in fact, derail a career over time.

BUILDING A PLAN TO DEAL WITH AN ASSHOLE BOSS

Okay, it's time to build your plan for dealing with a workplace asshole. First, I'll outline a plan to deal with an asshole boss. Then we'll look at a plan to deal with an ass-clown coworker. I want to start with bad bosses because, although bad coworkers are an annoyance, an exceedingly bad boss can create unmanageable stress.

Let's summarize our plan framework thus far: Take care of yourself: Anchor yourself in the encouragement of loved ones, and validate and prioritize what's important. Second, get in the right frame of mind: Unjack your brain so you can put stress-related emotions on the shelf, and weed out false choices. Third, do reality checks: Realistically assess the likelihood that the organization or asshole will change, and realistically assess your readiness for change.

Recall that in dealing with a workplace asshole there's a binary decision that you will need to consider: Do I stay or do I leave? Staying does not mean enduring or tolerating a terrible work environment. Nor does leaving mean having to take a step down in your career or moving somewhere you'd rather not go.

Framework for Dealing with Asshole Boss

What follows is a framework for evaluating your decision to stay or leave. Don't mistake this framework for a list of pros and cons. This is not meant to trade off the pluses and minuses of staying or leaving. The framework is meant to facilitate clarity and objectiveness in your decision-making.

Stay Considerations and Possible Implications

What do you want to achieve?

Experience: There may be long-term value from the short-term experiences you are gaining. For example, if you're working on a significant migration to a new technology platform: seeing this through to the end may prove valuable in advancing your career, either where you are or somewhere else.

Money: What short-term financial incentives or anticipated promotions are (honestly) on the horizon? Timing is everything. Sometimes the financial upside is worth sticking around for a bit. In the end, though, no amount of money is worth damaging your health or your relationships. This is important to keep in mind when long-term incentives are at play. There's a reason they're called *golden-handcuffs*. That said, I've known people who have walked away from six-figure incentives because it wasn't worth putting up with a toxic work environment created by an asshole.

Relationships: What connections do you have (or are on the horizon) that will help with your career, now and down the road? I like this saying: "Who you know will get you in the door, but it's what you know that will keep you there." Once you reach a certain level in your professional career, your next move will depend heavily on the relationships you have.

Leave Considerations and Possible Implications

Testing the Waters

How long will it take to find another job? Most folks underestimate how long it takes to find a job. Here's a quick view from inside the HR department.

Depending on the level of the job and internal politics it can take between 2 and 6 weeks for a job requisition to be created, reviewed, and approved. Then the job has to be posted, often internally and externally.

The posting process can run from 4 to 6 months, again depending on the job. Screening and identifying potential job candidates takes weeks to months. Then there are interviews, second interviews, compliance and affirmative-action check-offs: all before a job offer is ever crafted. A very short hiring process would be 3 to 4 months. A typical process would be 6 to 9 months. And if you are pulling down over six figures, plan on a 12-month search process.

If you are considering leaving your company here are a few points to consider. Relationships can help cut through the search process. Hiring is more art than science. Personally, I will put much more credibility on a reference from someone I respect than on a well-polished resume. Also, it's easier to find a job when you have a job. If at all possible, do not quit your job before you have another job in hand.

Marketable and Flexible: If it's been a while since you were in the job market you might have to knock the dust off your "selling" skills. Don't be timid about taking interviews for jobs that may not be your ideal. Consider the opportunity as a dress rehearsal for the job interview you really want. When that ideal interview comes along, be cool. Don't be over anxious. While the job opportunity will be the most important event for you (at this time), for the hiring manager finding the next candidate is one of several important tasks on their plate. Give the process time to work out.

Look before you leap (greener grass): The only thing worse than staying in a workplace with a flaming asshole, is leaving only to end up working with another (or worse) a-hole. Be careful that you're not so desperate to leave a rotten situation that you mistakenly find yourself in a worse state. Keep in mind that the decision to join a company is yours. Be selective in your decisions.

Here are some tips to help make sure your next job is as "asshat free" as possible. Since the company will check your references, it's only fair that you check theirs. Beyond understanding the financial and business health of a company, the real reference check will come from the employees. One method for gaining a pulse on employee perceptions regarding their company is sites like Glassdoor. Glassdoor is like Yelp on companies, and is a good barometer on the pros and cons, as viewed from those who work there.

The Reality Checks

What is reasonable to expect:

Change within the Company: Can I change roles or jobs inside my current company? Can I move to another department or division within my company and advance my career in a positive manner? Many organizations intentionally look to promote or move their employees around. Consider if there are other areas in your company where you can go. Sometimes, this may mean taking a lateral move. It may even mean taking a step back. These aren't bad moves as long as you have a thought-out plan. When planning your career, think chess, not checkers.

Change within you: The question here is, "How well can you protect yourself from the asshole?" There's no shame in acknowledging enough is enough. An executive who was dealing with a toxic workplace shared with me that she would stay until she had enough; she compiled enough money and had taken enough crap. When discerning your readiness to make a personal change, be sure to critically assess the strength of your ARSe immune system.

This framework is intentionally simple for one reason. The decision to stay or leave really isn't all that complicated. To be frank, if you've picked up this book, you instinctively know what you need to do. All you need is a framework to help your mind get to where your heart has been for a while. The question behind the question of whether to stay or leave is what to do once you have decided.

BUILDING A PLAN TO DEAL WITH AN ASSHOLE TEAMMATE

This book was written to help those suffering from ARSe draw on a straightforward framework to understand, assess, and deal with workplace assholes. While writing it, I drew heavily on my close friends and trusted colleagues for feedback, advice and insight. As writing proceeded, it was unsettling how often an ARSe sufferer would say to me, "Okay, Pete, you know something on this topic. In simple terms, tell me what to do." For months I struggled with crafting an ARSe emergency med-pack that would provide a quick, straightforward approach to dealing with a workplace asshole.

The Allure of an ARSe Emergency Med-Pack (Hard Facts)

As hard as I tried, I just couldn't build a meaningful, simple framework for an ARSe emergency med-pack. Every effort to do so was blocked by countless cautions and caveats. In the end I had to go back to my foundational belief: There are no easy answers for dealing with a workplace asshole. There are answers, but they don't fit into a neat three-step plan. I was forced to come to terms with some hard facts about ARSe:

Hard Fact 1: There Are Asshats Everywhere.

In every organization, team or department and at every level from individual team member to supervisor right up to the top leaders in a firm, you will find nasty, mean-spirited people.

Hard Fact 2: There Are No Easy Answers.

Because of the first fact, odds are fairly good that at some point in your life an asshole will enter your workplace and create havoc. It will suck! Dealing with such a person in your workplace will take thoughtful consideration and intentional planning. It will not be easy.

Hard Fact 3: You Did Nothing to Deserve the Grief You're Enduring.

No one should ever have to tolerate an asshole at work. The hard fact is this: If something is going to change, you are the one who will need to catalyze that change. You don't necessarily need to go down this path alone, but, then again, you may. Let me be as clear as I can: There will be a cost to you in confronting a bad actor in the workplace. Beyond the stress and anxiety that comes from the garbage such a person brings to the team, if you take up the mantle to change things, it will cost you. Sometimes the cost may simply be your time and effort.

Other times the cost may be your status, reputation, and stability in the firm. Only you can decide if that cost is worth it.

Framework for Dealing with Asshole Coworkers

Much the same as dealing with an asshole boss, your first step when building your plan to deal with an asshole coworker is to discern what kind of asshole is lurking in your workplace. Sometimes the coworker is simply an annoying prick. Others are flaming assholes.

Your second step to consider is the degree of disruption and damage this person is having on you, the team, and the company. How you answer these questions will provide valuable insight in building your plan. The following scenarios will help guide your planning and decisions[46]:

Level:	**Level 1—*Annoying Prick:*** Annoying pricks are folks who are so miserable with the world and their place in it that they make it their goal to create misery for others. They are perennial under performers who blame others for their lackluster results.
Impact:	For the most part an annoying prick's behavior is akin to that of a personality quirk or a lack of social etiquette. While interactions with their coworkers are awkward, you (and others) can keep your distance and avoid them.

---

[46] In the appendix I make a comparison between Jim Collins' Level 1 to 5 leaders to Level 1 to 5 Assholes.

Options: The question you need to ask is this: "Do you care enough about the annoying prick to make the effort in helping them see how their behavior is impacting others?" The bottom line is, do you try to help the person see and address their ineffective behavior? Even if you do try to help, keep in mind that they may not want your help, or they may not gain the awareness and make the adjustments needed to better navigate social interactions.

The biggest risk is your investment of time and effort. If you decide to help, your best approach is get another teammate to partner with you. Then the two of you should look to build a relationship with your coworker before you launch a litany of their social deficiencies. Telling a coworker "You suck" has less chance of making an impact than letting a friend know there are areas they can work on to improve interactions with their teammates.

Level: Level 2—*Frustrating Asshole:* These are assholes who rarely if ever take accountability for their results, often getting others to do their work, while they are quick to take credit for others' efforts. They have a strong sense of entitlement and are the last in and the first out.

Impact: These folks have a measurable negative impact on the team. It's clear that if their behavior goes unchecked, the team will degrade to the point of dysfunction, perhaps resulting in diminished team performance or even defections of team members.

Options: In this situation the best course of action is to speak with the team boss. Again, going to the boss with a few of your fellow teammates can be very helpful, if only in dissuading the boss from thinking the problem is just between you and the asshole. There is clearly a risk though: A risk that the boss mismanages the feedback you share and tells the person that you (and others) have a problem with them. I've seen this happen with grave consequences as the person makes a *list* of those they feel are out to get them. The state of the team goes from bad to worse.

However, the risk to the team of inaction often outweighs the risks of further alienating the jerk. If all that happens is that the person knows that their asinine behavior is "on-the-record," this can be a good thing. If the team boss leads well, the person will realize that their behavior will need to change or additional actions will be taken—up to and including being removed from the team/ organization.

Level:

Note: Levels 3, 4 and 5 are combined because these asshole coworkers need to be considered in a group.

Level 3—*Throwback Asshole:* These folks exude an arrogant sense of superiority that is often fueled by perceived "special" relationships or personal friendships and alliances with those in leadership roles.

Level 4—*Sophisticated Asshole:* They place a high value on their political and organizational savvy. They know how to read prevailing opinion and are adept at agreeing with everything yet standing for nothing. The most significant thing to understand is that sophisticated assholes react decisively to threats to their position and power and to disloyalty within the ranks.

Level 5—*Flaming Asshole:* This person exhibits a predictable pattern of callous, manipulative, arrogant, and self-absorbed behavior from which a toxic and harmful workplace environment emerges. They are given to bullying and intimidating others into following their suggestions and ideas.

Impact:

The impact on individuals and teams from asshole coworkers in levels 3, 4, and 5 is readily visible. This impact includes an 8% decrease in team work effort, a 38% decrease in their work quality, and a 63% increase in lost time avoiding the asshole.

Options: Dealing with people in levels 3, 4, and 5 is very difficult–and why an ARSe med-pack is nearly impossible to craft. This difficulty is compounded when the asshole coworker is given to bullying and/or intimidating fellow teammates. The very best approach for dealing with coworkers at levels 3 to 5 is to use the framework outlined earlier for dealing with asshole bosses. Even though the coworker isn't your boss, trust me when I say; "They believe they are." Build and execute your plan for these levels of ass-clown coworkers the same way you would if they were your boss. It may be overkill but having a stronger than necessary plan is much better than the alternative.

WORKING YOUR PLAN: STAYING OR LEAVING

Whether you decide to stay or leave you need to have a plan.

Staying

If you believe your best option is to stay, then I encourage you to re-read Chapter 7 and focus closely on *Strengthening your ARSe Immune System* and *Preventing the spread of ARSe;* particularly in the following areas:

Setting Boundaries

Be clear in your mind what you consider acceptable behavior and what crosses the line. Then communicate this to the workplace asshole. You don't need to be belligerent or over demanding. Simply state with clarity and calmness what is and what is not okay.

For example:

What's Okay	What I will not tolerate
High expectations	Unreasonable demands
Critical assessments	Demeaning or offensive comments/behavior
Challenging assignments	Verbal, physical, or psychological abuse

Be Friendly, but Not Friends.

Remember you don't have to become an asshole in order to deal with one. I like this advice: Be friendly, but not friends. Remember, assholes have no friends; they have acquaintances, whom they exploit as it serves their purpose. Be mindful that an asshat will use their psychopathic trait to lure you into to thinking a "relationship" exists. Don't fall for it. Be on guard not to put yourself in a situation in which you begin to rely on an asshole's trustworthiness or integrity. They will eventually turn on you when it suits their purpose.

Keep a Journal.

Earlier I pointed out the cathartic value of keeping a journal. Journaling can provide a healthy avenue to release tension and frustration. It gives you a touchstone to go back and reflect on how you navigated a difficult time in your life.

Equally important, however, is the advantage in keeping detailed notes of each poor encounter you've had with a workplace asshole, especially if they are your boss. Providing thoughtfully documented details about the behaviors and mistreatments you've experienced can be a credible resource should you eventually need to go to HR or if you opt to contact a lawyer.

Standing Up to Bullies—Speaking Up.

There will be times when you simply have to stand your ground. At that point, it's critical to distinguish between confrontation and providing feedback. The term *feedback* gets used a lot these days, usually with modifiers attached such as *positive, real-time,* or, my favorite *feedforward.* So what is feedback anyway? A hoity-toity definition would be:

> Feedback is sharing observations stemming from personal experiences that either help affirm actions that are positive or create space to consider adjusting actions that are ineffective.

In normal language feedback is about letting the people you interact with know how they're doing. It is about encouraging someone when they've done something well and offering helpful advice when something wasn't so great. There are two key premises connected with feedback:

> First, for most individuals, and in most cultures, a good relationship and rapport are necessary for feedback to be effective. Without a good relationship, feedback is at best a hollow flattery or at worst, an unwelcome criticism. Second, there is a clear and validated understanding that feedback is both sought and welcomed.

Confrontation, on the other hand, is about putting an issue on the table with someone you believe will be unreceptive or even hostile towards your opinions, views, or objections. Before you even offer your insights, you know there is going to be some level of conflict. The classic approach to confrontation is to go toe-to-toe with your adversary, as illustrated in Mark Goulston's encounter with F. Lee Bailey during the OJ Simpson trial. During the trail Bailey all but accused Goulston of "coaching" a key prosecution witness. Goulston describes what happened in the meeting:

For several minutes, Bailey said things like, "Dr. Goulston, we don't know exactly why you're here, but we know you've been here for most of the trial." As [Bailey] talked I just looked him squarely in the eyes. Instead of saying or doing anything, I simply blinked occasionally.

Finally, another attorney looked at me and said, "Mark, you haven't said anything." At which point I said, "He hasn't asked me a question." I went right back to looking Bailey in the eye, and he flinched slightly.

Next Bailey asked if I'd brainwashed or drugged…[the witness] or somehow done something to prepare him for his testimony… Bailey was hoping I'd panic and say something stupid he could twist or distort. Even when you are innocent, it's pretty intimidating to be grilled by F. Lee Bailey. However, I had the advantage of seeing through his game: his goal was to disarm, frustrate, and then outrage me, so I'd lose my cool.

So when…[Bailey] asked if I'd drugged or brainwashed…[a key witness]—an outrageous question—I waited a full count of seven and then cleared my throat. At that point everyone in the room was waiting breathlessly to hear what I'd say. I counted to another full count of seven, and said to Bailey, "Excuse me, Mr. Bailey, my mind wandered over the past few minutes. Can you please repeat what you said?"

[Bailey]…was absolutely dumbfounded. How could I dare find the world's most intimidating lawyer so boring as to become distracted? And after that…[Bailey] backed down.

Most of us are conflict avoidant. Depending on where you live or grew up, this avoidance can be more or less pronounced. Because my dad was in the Army, I've lived in Europe, Asia, and various places in the U.S. I could take several pages describing how people in Europe and Asia approach conflict, but for now we'll stick with the U.S. From my experience, living and working across the United States, I would say the folks in the northeast are fairly straightforward about telling people what they think (that's code for "They are not shy"). In the south, criticism usually includes a "Bless your heart!" West coast folks spend so much time hanging out with people just like them it's hard sometimes to know what's a criticism and what's a compliment. Finally, folks in the middle of the U.S. are so polite and respectful that they will rarely criticize someone to their face; they tell everyone else but not the person who needs to hear it.

Regardless of where you live, the notion of confronting a workplace a-hole is likely very intimidating. Rather than address the issue straight on, we back off, with the end result being that "whole teams are held hostage by a single toxic employee whom everyone is afraid to confront." Just know this, deciding to stay means at some point you will you have to confront a workplace a-hole. When this time comes, I have seen and experienced the following approaches to be helpful:

Practice respectful dissent: Keep your cool and be calm. Don't intentionally set out to antagonize the asshole, but don't take their crap either. Stand your ground without losing your composure. You can hold and communicate a dissenting view in a professional manner. For example, if your boss is pushing a view that's demeaning, disrespectful, or downright harmful, consider saying, "I see this differently" or "I find that unsettling." Then explain your view with clarity and brevity (brevity is key here). Next, allow the boss to react, which will most likely be true to their asinine behavior. Afterwards if the boss's position is one you can accept calmly say, "You're the boss and I defer to your direction."[47] If the boss has crossed the line, respond calmly, "I'm still uncomfortable with this. I'll need some time to consider this fully."

---

[47] There's a great line in the movie "Bridge of Spies" when accused Russian spy Rudolf Abel says, "The boss may not always be right, but they are always the boss."

The most important point in respectful dissent is this: "Don't be a victim, and don't be a hero." If you come off as vulnerable, the asshole will walk over you time and time again. On the other hand, you may daydream about really telling off your boss, or you may fantasize about pouring a can of soda over your coworker's head. Don't do it. No matter how much your teammates may admire and appreciate your actions, the momentary joy is short-lived and you'll likely be forced to look for another job.

Know the leverage points. Be mindful of the leavers at play. Clearly your boss has leavers to throw: your job security, pay, promotions, and reputation. You likewise have leavers: your expertise on key processes and systems, your impact on your boss's reputation, and the impact on the company's reputation should you seek outside legal counsel.

Navigate the message with HR or other senior leaders. Keep in mind that sometimes there are conversations you *need* to have in order to get to the conversation you *want* to have. When speaking with HR or other senior leaders about the workplace asshole, craft your message carefully. Before you get to the conversation you want to have about how the person is creating a hostile work environment, you have to engage the specific incidents that are creating the hostile environment. So navigate the message and speak to each lousy event as they occur. Build your case and keep your journal up to date. Then, when you bring up the conversation about a hostile work environment, you have a pattern of behavior versus one isolated event.

A Word of Caution

Be mindful to measure carefully how much and how hard you push back on the workplace asshole. Try your very best not to piss them off or create an enemy. This saying is true and worth keeping top of mind: **If someone likes you they will go out of their way to help you in a time of need. But if an ass–clown hates you they will make it their life's mission to screw you over.**

Leaving

Although actually leaving is tricky and must be navigated with great care, deciding to leave is fairly straightforward. There are a few rules to follow should you decide to leave.

Rule 1: Don't Tell Anyone Your Business

Deciding to leave can, in itself, create a great sense of relief. Just knowing there is an end in sight is so fantastic that you're going to want to tell everybody you know, even before you've started your job search. Don't do it. I've known ARSe suffers who shared with their coworkers their decision to leave, mistakenly believing everything was in confidence. Here's a saying we all would do well to keep top of mind: "A secret is something that is shared one person at a time." Organizations are really a tangled web of gossip-riddled grapevines. No matter how much you want to believe a trusted colleague will hold your confidence, it's not going to happen. And eventually the rumor reaches the wrong ears, and things go from bad to worse. So *don't tell anyone your business*. When you have a job offer you've accepted, then let folks know.

Rule 2: Don't Burn Bridges

When you have an opportunity to leave the company, avoid the temptation to tell them where they can put their lousy job. Don't do it. Fight the urge to get the last word in so you exact a pound of flesh for the grief you've endured. Never burn a bridge you may need to cross back over someday. Who knows what might happen? The asshole may leave, more reasonable leadership come in, and someone recalls a great employee from back in the day (you).

You might ask, "How do I let the company know how bad things are?" "How can I help the poor folks who are left behind?" Trust me, as the head of HR for many years, I can assure you the company already knows how bad things are, they're just not doing anything about it. Your insights will not shed new light on things. If an organization is really interested in knowing why people are leaving, there are effective vehicles they can use beyond input from an exit interview.

If the company (typically HR) asks for an exit interview and questions you about why you are leaving, just tell them that leaving was a very hard decision, but you've been afforded a unique opportunity in another firm. Tell HR how much you've grown and learned while there. Show that you value and respect the company and will miss everyone dearly. Then once you get home wash out your mouth with a dark beer and a shot of single malt scotch.

When and How to go to HR

While I've worked in and lead an HR function for some time, my career includes stints in Information Technology, Engineering, Marketing and Product Development. From these experiences I can say with conviction that leading an HR function is one of the most rewarding and frustrating roles I've ever had. The rewarding side comes from partnering with business leaders in creating meaningful experiences for employees, which in turn drive significant impact to business results.

The actions many organizations take regarding their employees reveal a belief that they regard people as little more than a commodity--something that can be bought, sold, and traded with ease.

Here's a little-known fact When an employee is having the worst day of their life, either because of a personal/family illness or the passing of a loved one, the first call the employee makes is to HR.

The care and compassion HR professionals extend to employees and their families is nothing short of inspiring. To be honest, there are so many frustrating days in HR that they outweigh the good days. In talking with other HR leaders around the U.S., I've found a shared frustration with the lack of appreciation for the role of HR. Let me be clear. This frustration goes much deeper than a lack of respect for the HR function itself. The heart of the matter for many HR professionals is a sense that while nearly every company will say their employees are their most valuable resource, very few organizations actually live this belief.[48] The actions many organizations take regarding their employees reveal a belief that they regard people as little more than a commodity—something that can be bought, sold, and traded with ease.

You can easily see where a company stands on valuing its employees by looking at a few key indicators such as:

- The ratio of officers that watch over the company's money (e.g., CFO, CAO, and Treasurer) compared to the number of officers that watch over the company's people.
- Where HR is positioned in the organization structure. Does HR report into the CEO or is HR rolled under an administrative, operations or legal function?
- HR's position of influence. Does HR actively and directly participate at the executive and board level, or is HR assumed under a broad array of functional updates?
- In addition to enterprise metrics such as budget, revenue, customer, and shareholder, what employee-related metrics are tracked at an enterprise level?

Consider this: Does your organization know as much about their employees as it does about inventory turns and equipment maintenance? Is HR a valued thought partner or does HR function more like the old-fashioned personnel department, simply overseeing hiring and firing?

Frankly, I'm sick and tired of the thoughtless excuses for why HR is relegated to second-class status. Tell me if the following sounds familiar:

---

[48] The head of HR for a Fortune 500 company shared a story about a commercial they ran showcasing their values and public service. Several executives where filmed sharing their individual views. When the commercial ran, the HR head was featured saying, "At our company, there is nothing more important than our people." After the commercial aired the CEO called the HR leader into her office and asked, "Can we really say this?" "Isn't this true?" the HR leader replied. "That's what I'm asking." the CEO said. "Is this true?"

- *Every officer and every leader is accountable for maintaining a focus on our employees. We don't need HR doing this.* That's true. As true as the fact that every officer and leader has accountability for budget and revenue. So is caring for your money more important than caring for your employees?

- *HR needs to do the blocking and tackling before they can be a valued thought partner.* Absolutely true. If you lack the confidence in the capability of your HR team to deliver on the fundamentals, then throw the rascals to the curb and get HR folks who can.

- *HR needs to earn its seat at the table.* Yes and, equally important, your employees deserve an HR function that has the voice and influence to ensure talent is part of an ongoing strategic conversation.

Now let's return to our subject. When should you go to HR?

Why did I just unleash a diatribe on HR? Because it's helpful context when considering if and when you should go to HR about a workplace asshole. In an ideal world HR would be one of the first places you'd go. But ask yourself this: "Why is HR here?" "What is their key function?" The answer varies widely. In really good companies, the mission of HR is to make sure the organization has the workforce it needs, both for today and tomorrow. HR is the caretaker to ensure employees are fully engaged and hold a belief that they have a bright future with the firm.

In other organizations, HR's role is to do everything needed to keep the company out of the courtroom and off the front page. Regardless of any banners, plaques, or posters in the HR department, they give maniacal adherence towards the "company line." My personal view is this, I don't need a stinking rulebook to tell me what the right thing to do is. All I need a rulebook for is guidance on how to do the right thing the right way.[49]

With these thoughts in mind, here's a few thoughts I would share with a person I'm coaching concerning if, when, and how to approach HR regarding a workplace asshole:

First, if you feel threatened or unsafe because of someone acting badly in the workplace, even in the slightest way, make sure you share your concerns formally. Go to your boss first, unless they are the reason you feel unsafe. If so, then go directly to HR. Be clear and specific in detailing what you've experienced and why you feel your safety is at risk.

A good HR person and an attentive boss will take detailed notes on your concerns and ask you to review and validate that they have captured your input correctly. If this doesn't happen, then take the initiative to commit your experiences to paper and formally give this to your boss and HR. Finally, you should ask your boss or HR to outline the next steps they will take. And you should ask what next steps you should take as well.

Every HR professional I've known and worked with understands the seriousness of earnestly running to ground every concern raised about workplace safety. Businesses likewise understand their obligation (and liability) to ensure a safe workplace.

Second, if the workplace asshole is a coworker, then first go to your boss. If nothing happens over time, then go to HR. Make sure you provide clear and concise feedback. The more details the better. It would also be helpful to have a few colleagues accompany you to HR and corroborate your input.

Third, if the workplace asshole is your boss, then tread lightly. If

---

[49] I was 3 weeks into an HR leadership role at a new firm when the vice president of marketing interrupted my team meeting to ask, "Hey Dr. Pete, what's our policy on buying flowers for an employee whose mom passed away?" I honestly couldn't believe the question, and the fact the VP just bolted into my meeting. My first thought was, "Why on earth do we need a policy on this?" But my answer was, "What do you want to do?" The VP wasn't ready to own the decision, so they paused before eventually saying, "I want to buy the flowers." "Then buy the flowers." I said. "If you need to know where to get flowers or how to expense the costs, I can have someone get back to you." "No, I got that," the VP replied, then left the meeting.

your boss is lower in the organization, then first go to your boss's manager. If you're in a company with long-tenured employees, then be on guard for the "old boy" network. Buddies will look after buddies. If you see no visible action, then bounce your concern to HR. Again, have clear and concise feedback and bring along coworkers to back up your concerns.

Fourth, if the workplace asshat is an executive (one or two levels from the CEO or the CEO themselves), be extremely careful. It is very difficult to motivate an organization to take formal action against an executive. I've seen executives get away with some of the most egregious behaviors because they are seen either as an expert in a critical area or a rainmaker in delivering key results, and there can be fears about negative reactions from the public or markets to their "unfavorable" exit. In my years dealing with bad leaders, I've only seen top executives exited from the company a few times. Some notable experiences I've encountered were:

- A CEO who was such a flaming asshole (level 5) that nearly their entire executive team quit and, over the course of three months several large customers moved to competitors.

- An executive who was a known womanizer with subordinates. The last straw came when the executive propositioned an external sales consultant, suggesting he would make a significant purchase in exchange for sexual favors.

- A vice president who was so abusive that an employee had an emotional breakdown. Their spouse subsequently retained a lawyer and sued the firm. Rather than go to court the company settled for an undisclosed amount and the VP left the firm.

Can you speak up anonymously?

The fear of retaliation is the single greatest reason most ARSe suffers do not speak up. Who can blame them? Their situation is tough enough without giving a workplace asshole a reason to lash out. So, here's the rub: Can you really let HR know what's going on without it coming back to bite you in the butt? I shared earlier that as it relates to coworkers there's no such thing as a confidential conversation, but is that true when talking to HR? In truth, there's no formal code of ethics for the HR profession: no client-patient confidentiality agreement like you have with doctors, lawyers, or counselors. That's because HR is a business function, not an employee advocacy group. That said, most HR professionals hold themselves to a high standard for keeping sensitive information confidential. The problem arises with the uncertainty between you and your HR professional about what should be considered confidential information. When asked, "Can I share something with you confidentially, off the record?" a good HR professional will respond, "It depends on what you share."

Here is a bit more "inside HR" to help you navigate your interaction. Be mindful that HR is not the place where you want to vent and blow off steam. The work of the HR professional is one dramatic soap opera. So don't add to the drama when you share the issues you are having with a workplace asshole. Remember, be clear and concise. If you have a journal, summarize your experiences. Second, when you go to HR, make sure your own house is in order. That means you need to understand your own credibility will be called into review. If you're an employee in good standing, you've achieved solid performance ratings, and you have delivered quality and timely results, then your input will carry weight.

However, if you have a less than stellar track record with the company, then your complaints may fall on deaf ears. This stinks, but trust me when I tell you that any blemishes on your performance history will undermine the credibility of your input. If you have a track record of underperformance, the suspicion will be you're simply trying to undermine your boss's leadership.

The goal in taking your concerns to HR is threefold; (1) bring awareness of the toxic conditions being created by a workplace asshole; (2) receive advice on what you should be doing; and (3) receive affirmation that your concerns are heard, taken seriously, and follow-up will be forthcoming.

Here are some reactions you may get when you approach HR:

- *"We know":* The chance is better than good that the folks in HR are already aware of the situation. Honestly, there's very little company drama HR doesn't already know. They know who the bad actors are, who's having inappropriate office romances, who are the chief butt-kissers, and who's working the system to move up the ladder. But knowing and doing something about it are two different things.

- *Blank stares:* When you share your information, pay close attention to how the HR professional responds. Most HR folks have lousy poker-faces. If the HR person doesn't respond empathically to what you're saying, pause and ask, "Have you heard this already?" If they say yes, then respond, "May I ask what is being done?" The response you get will line up with what I shared earlier. If the asshole is a coworker or a lower level leader, then HR should either be conducting an investigation to gather more facts or may be initiating a "performance improvement plan" with the person and their boss. If the asshole is a senior executive, do not be surprised if nothing is being done at all.

- *"So what would you like to see happen?":* If HR throws this line at you it's either a smokescreen from a lackluster HR professional or it's a passive-aggressive response from an aggravated HR person who's at their wits' end, just like you. Avoid saying you want the asshat covered in honey and tied to an anthill. Your best response to the question, "What would you like to see happen?" would be something like: "a professional and respectful workplace."

- *Radar on for code words:* HR professionals are trained to have an ear turned to key words and phrases. Here are just a few: *hostile workplace, unsafe, violent, abusive, discrimination.* Don't throw these words around carelessly. Used strategically and intentionally, though, you will be certain to get HR's attention.

Wrap up your visit with HR by asking "What's next?" Ask for advice about what you should be doing. Then ask HR what their next steps will be. It's also fine to ask when you should expect to hear back from them. Bear in mind that it is always a good idea to keep a record of your meeting with HR, noting the date and time of the meeting and what was said. Finally, here is my last "inside HR" thought. HR lives by this motto, "Transparency does not mean full disclosure." There may very well be solid progress underway to deal with the workplace asshole, but HR can't go into the details with you.

When to Talk to a Lawyer

Here's something you know but may not think about all that often: Your company either employs or retains lawyers. What this means in the world of HR is that every employment action ever taken and nearly every policy, guideline, or procedure has in one fashion or another been vetted by legal counsel. Regrettably, that's the way it has to be. We live in such a litigious society that companies are dangerously exposed if they're not constantly consulting an attorney. It shouldn't be surprising that many HR functions and in-house lawyers actively look to stay current with the ever-changing employment laws. To this end, companies such as the National Employment Law Institute[50] have surfaced to educate attorneys and HR professionals. So before you go off and hire a lawyer to help you deal with your workplace asshat, consider this sobering fact. Currently in the United States there are no laws requiring your boss be nice, kind, or fair: only that the boss not treat you differently because of your age, sex, race, religion, national

---

[50] http://www.neli.org/

Currently in the United States there are no laws requiring your boss be nice, kind, or fair: only that the boss not treat you differently because of your age, sex, race, religion, national origin, or disability.

origin, or disability. If your boss is an equal opportunity asshole, it may be very hard to win a legal case just because they're a bad person.

If you've done all you can to give your company and HR the opportunity to deal with your workplace asshole, and you're struggling with whether to talk with a lawyer, my advice is talk to a lawyer. Again, you can bet that your company is talking to a lawyer, so there's no harm in asking for legal advice. I once asked an ARSe suffer who had connected with a lawyer if they found it helpful. Their simple reply: "Absolutely."

Yet finding a good lawyer can be a bit of a maze. The only way to navigate the maze is to roll up your sleeves and look for a law firm that specializes in labor and employee relations law. Don't use the same lawyer who helped close on your house. Look for a lawyer who knows employment law. Look for ratings on the firm and their track record. Finally, be sure to find out the up-front costs. Some lawyers may agree to work on contingency (meaning they get paid if you get paid). This is not a standard practice, so make sure you ask up front what costs will be involved. This is a personal bias on my part, but I want to know when and how often my lawyer is on the clock.

Let me offer one last sobering fact. Unless you have a solid piece of evidence that shows your boss has it out for you, in the end the matter will come down to a few key items. Can a lawyer in a discovery phase uncover a pattern of malicious intent by your boss to create a hostile workplace? If not, your lawyer will most likely need to depose or subpoena your workplace friends and colleagues in order to build a case. What this means is that in order for you to win your day in court, you may be asked to put the job security of your friends and colleagues at risk. Again, I know that this stinks, but this scenario plays out more often than you would think.

Chapter 9: What Organizations Should Do About Workplace Assholes

Earlier, I outlined the business impact related to workplace assholes, including decreased performance, increase in lost time, and stress-related illnesses. So why do companies tolerate toxic employees in their workplace? As I've said, there are all kinds of reasons that those leading organizations turn a blind eye toward people who act badly in the workplace. The asshole might be a key subject matter expert that the company believes it can't afford to lose, or they are a rainmaker who generates remarkable sales or business results, or the person is a perceived as an "untouchable" executive, someone who appears to be protected by a wall of high-ranking cronies.

If an organization genuinely wants to create an asshole-free workplace then those leading the organization would do well to address the same questions I challenge assholes themselves to consider in the appendix: Do you know? Do you care?

A company is not measured by what they say in their values or ethics statements but by what it does each day to create meaningful experiences that instill worthwhile beliefs for their employees.

If by chance this book has found its way into the hands of those leading organizations, I implore you to take the following to heart.

THE BOTTOM LINE: CULTURE

If you have the honor of leading an organization, then I ask you this very direct and frank question, "Do you care about the quality of the culture in your company and the effectiveness of its leaders?" This is not a trick question. Of course, company leaders care about culture and leadership, but the distance between *caring* and *action* can be miles. A common reason I've witnessed for inaction in dealing with people who behave badly in the workplace is a belief that the problem is a giant can of worms with no straightforward answer. In reality, the first step in creating an asshole-free workplace is very straightforward. Let me explain.

Over the years I've have the privilege of partnering with a several remarkable leaders who were committed to building a strong and healthy culture in their organizations.[51] These leaders were clear in defining a meaningful culture for their organization, and they intentionally created experiences that moved the company towards this desired culture.

Every organization has its own distinct culture. Even if the company doesn't have an intentional focus on its culture, a distinct culture exists nonetheless. We can cite the many positive results that stem from defining and developing a strong and healthy corporate culture, but perhaps illustrating the results from a poor organizational culture would better make my point.

I was connected with the space program when we lost seven crew members aboard Challenger. A few of the folks that worked for us watched over the children of the astronauts we lost while their spouses flew from Houston to Kennedy. Beneath the scientific reasons why we lost Challenger was a fundamental culture that did not allow or encourage people to raise concerns up the ladder so that important issues were adequately addressed.

Soon after Challenger, NASA began an intentional effort to reshape its culture so that all ideas and concerns would be heard. A key focus of the culture work was to encourage asking tough and uncomfortable questions. What was interesting in this work was that NASA was not looking to instill a new culture but to return to the culture that emerged after the Apollo 1 fire that took the lives of Grissom, White, and Chaffee. Few people know that the phrase *"A Failure of Imagination,"* which was used as the title for the 9/11

---

[51] Honestly, the volume of books about culture could fill a moderate-sized library. In simple terms, we can define culture as this: Culture is what a group of people believe and how these beliefs influence how they behave. Culture is what we think and how we act. For example, if I believe my boss is a valued partner in my career growth, I will be inclined to seek my boss' help if I want to pursue a career opportunity outside our department. If I believe my boss is more interested in their own function and personal career, then I will be less likely to let them know I'm pursuing opportunities outside the department.

Commission Report, was spoken by Frank Borman when asked for his assessment of the root cause of the Apollo 1 fire. After Apollo 1, the culture at NASA evolved dramatically. Tough and uncomfortable questions could readily be asked, and answers were required to be provided before mission-critical functions could advance. One NASA senior engineer shared with me that they actually held the launch of an Apollo mission because he could not readily verify the cure date of the rubber in a spacesuit boot in the pre-launch check.

While many inside and outside NASA applauded the post-Challenger culture effort, the energy was short-lived. Before any lasting progress was made, new leadership stepped in at NASA—leadership that didn't believe culture could be seen or measured, so the effort was stopped. Then, 17 years later, we lost the Columbia crew. I had moved on by then, but friends in the space program I spoke with shared a sad sense of déjà vu. No one asked out loud the question on everyone's mind. Watching video of the launch, ice could clearly be seen striking the edge of the wing, but as the orbiter circled the earth, no one said, "Put on a suit. Go for a walk. Check out the panels."

Organizational culture, not personal character, influences how people behave.

For anyone who doesn't believe culture is everything, I can give you the names of the families and coworkers of two Shuttle crews who would strongly disagree. One of the sobering facts of life I've learned over the years is this: Organizational culture, not personal character, influences how people behave. If you don't want assholes to reign havoc in your organization, then care enough about your culture to create an asshole-free workplace. The first step is to define the expectations of effective leadership and what behaviors will not be tolerated.

DEAL WITH ASSHOLES EARLY

Organizations that are serious about creating a culture that doesn't tolerate assholes will boldly take on the following actions.

- Ask employees for feedback on how things are going. This can be in the form of on-going engagement surveys, focus groups, or regular town halls. After employees give this feedback, take action.

- Seek upward feedback from employees about how effectively their boss is leading. This is not a "Do you like your boss?" opinion poll. This is clear and direct feedback on key effectiveness measures of leadership. For example: Does your boss seek your input on decisions that impact you and the work you do? Does your boss effectively deal with poor performance on your team? Do you have input in defining goals and objectives for you and your team?

- Find out why employees leave. To be sure not every employee departure is cause for concern. There are all kinds of good reasons people leave, but don't guess at this. Find out the real reason why employees are leaving. A technique I've used is, rather than asking departing employees why they are leaving, ask the employee's colleagues. Colleagues know why their friend left, and they are equally as insightful about why/if they, themselves, might leave. So ask them. If you see trends that departures are because of poor management or leadership, address this quickly.

Organizations that are serious about creating a culture that doesn't tolerate people behaving badly will hold their leaders accountable for how they lead, while weeding out workplace assholes regardless at what level they spring up.

Chapter 10: Recovering From ARSe

In outlining how to treat asshole related stress, I defined the first priority as taking care of yourself. Key here is finding encouragement from a "special someone" in your life. Someone who will invest their time and energy to extend you warmth, kindness, and compassion, and who will walk alongside you as you develop and execute your plan to deal with a workplace asshole. As research in neuroscience has advanced, we have come to understand that having a special someone in our lives not only helps us in dealing with a person behaving badly in the workplace, but also plays a critical role in recovering from ARSe. This is because being close to someone, having strong meaningful relationships provides us a safe space to gain awareness about how we feel, and, in turn, to make sense of a confusing experience. Let's briefly explore the neuroscience involved in recovering from ARSe.

HOW OUR BRAINS RESPOND TO AND RECOVER FROM STRESS

When we're in a state of high stress, such as the unrelenting stress of working with or for an asshole, our brains release high levels of memory-blocking hormones. In a sense, we have a bit of short-term amnesia about the details of the stressful experience. Another thing that happens when we encounter difficult times is our brain reframes the experiences into a less stressful story. While this helps us survive a painful experience in the short term, our brains don't entirely ignore the stressful experience. Rather, they establish an implicit "encoding" of the experience and tucks it away into a quiet corner.

So, it's really important that once the asshole is out of our lives that we address and attend to this quiet corner of painful memories. Otherwise, over time, sometimes at the most vulnerable moment, these

> **When we're in a state of high stress, such as the unrelenting stress of working with or for an asshole, our brains release high levels of memory-blocking hormones.**

experiences may resurface, and the ARSe suffer may find himself or herself reliving the original stressful experience. Let me use an example to illustrate how this happens.

Dr. Siegel tells the story of Bruce, who was his patient at a Veterans Administration hospital. On his first day at the VA hospital, Dr. Siegel found Bruce hiding under his bed. Before the doctor could get his bearings, Bruce grabbed his ankles and pulled him under the bed. Then Bruce shoved a broom handle in Siegel's hands and shouted, "Shoot them if they come to get us!" Bruce was having a flashback. A flashback has nothing to do with remembering an experience. It is actually your brain reliving, real and in the moment, a stressful/traumatic experience from your past. Dr. Siegel explains what was occurring in Bruce's mind.

> The hippocampus region in our brains works closely with the other limbic areas, such as the fear-generating amygdala, to connect the details of our experiences with the emotional tone and meaning of these events. The left side of our hippocampus manages linguistic and factual knowledge; the right side organizes the building blocks of our life's stored memory relative to topic and time. All of this hippocampal work makes the search engine of memory retrieval more efficient. We can think of the hippocampus as the master puzzle piece assembler, which draws together the separate pieces of images and sensations of our memory into a "story" we can both relate to and communicate to others.

Let me repeat this because it's really important. During times of high stress our brains go into survival mode by releasing memory-blocking hormones and reframing the experiences into something less stressful. The problem with this short-term survival strategy is that while our memory is blocked, our hippocampus has, in fact, encoded the experience in the deep recesses of our memory. Unless and until we wrestle with these latent memories, we may struggle to fully recover from ARSe, and we may find it difficult to truly trust our coworkers and operate with our defenses always heightened. This is why having someone in your life to help you navigate these difficult memories is so important in recovering from ARSe. Here too, we have some remarkable research that affirms this key point.

THE SECRET TO LIFE (AND RECOVERING FROM ARSE)

From a neuroscience perspective we understand that when we have someone in our life who is totally connected with us, it's more than that this person simply "gets us"; it's that they "know us." They know how we think; they understand what bothers us. We can be open and honest with them and feel assured that they will always love and accept us. Recall from Chapter 7 that a key priority to treating ARSe is to keep in mind what's important. It would seem that Curly's Law[52] is a real thing: "The secret to life is one thing. Find that out, and nothing else matters."

All too often I hear noted behaviorists and motivational speakers extol the virtue of having a positive mental attitude to overcome difficult times in our lives. It's as if they're telling someone who is in one of the darkest places of their life to simply keep a stiff upper lip, think happy thoughts, and all will be fine. With great respect to my friends and colleagues in behavioral science, recovery from workplace assholes is not about having a positive mental attitude (PMA). Recovery from ARSe (from any of life's heartbreaks) is greatly enhanced by having positive meaningful relationships (PMRs): relationships that help you make sense of rotten experiences, craft a meaningful story, and build a sustainable legacy of assuredness.

The impact of PMRs in navigating and recovering from life's trials and troubles is clearly evident in a 75+ year Harvard study on adult development. Since 1938, researchers have studyied over 700 men (and more recently their spouses) with the goal of understanding the psychosocial variables and biological processes that influence health

---

[52] From the movie City Slickers

and well-being. The study focused on two groups of men: 268 Harvard graduates from the classes of 1939 through 1944, and 456 disadvantaged men who grew up in poor and troubled inner-city neighborhoods of Boston.

The uniqueness of the Harvard study cannot be overstated. For more than seven decades researchers studied these men as they grew from teenagers into their 80s and 90s. Some of these men, from both the Harvard group and the disadvantage group, went on to be doctors, lawyers, and businessmen. Some rose to high ranks, some fell in the other direction. One participant in the study went on to be the President of the United States.[53] From each participant, insights were drawn from interviews, medical records, and, more recently, brain scans.

According to Robert Waldinger, current director of the study, the results from the Harvard research should cause us all to pause and take note:

The single most important factor that influences health and recovery from ARSe is having good relationships in our lives.

And the converse is equally clear: Loneliness is toxic to our health and well-being. More specifically, as

researchers looked at the factors throughout the years that strongly influenced health and well-being, they found that relationships with friends, and especially spouses, were a major one. The people in the strongest relationships were protected against chronic disease, mental illness, and memory decline, even if those relationships had many ups and downs.

---

[53] John F Kennedy

The impact of loneliness on health was highlighted in Cigna's 2018 research report. Here is an excerpt from the summary of Cigna's report:

Approximately 1 in 6 adults in the U.S. suffer from a mental health condition, and research has noted that mental health issues are one of the most rapidly increasing causes of long-term illness. When examining the different issues affecting people with mental health conditions, there is a consistent part of the pathology: they also suffer from loneliness. Loneliness has the same impact on mortality as smoking 15 cigarettes a day, making it even more dangerous than obesity.

Cigna's study revealed the following insights:
- Generation Z (adults ages 18–22) and Millennials (adults ages 23–37) are lonelier and claim to be in worse health than older generations.
- Students have higher loneliness scores than retirees.
- There was no major difference between men and women and no major difference between races when it came to average loneliness scores.

The Final Word on ARSe

It seems fitting that I end this book where I began. Early on I defined the General Theory of Assholes by drawing from work published in 2001 on the General Theory of Love. I was drawn to the author's summary: "Who we are and who we become depends, in part, on whom we love."

I am remarkably blessed to have that "special someone" in my life, someone who has walked with me through life's highs and lows for more than 35 years. Someone who is an expert encourager. Someone who has provided me a safe, nonjudgmental space to gain clarity about how I feel and in turn to make sense of rotten, senseless experiences.

Of all the lessons I've learned from studying organizational proctology and from coaching ARSe suffers, the most important lesson is this:

The key to navigating life's highs and lows and building a healthy and happy life is dependent on who we love and who loves us.

It would be the most profound omission if I did not acknowledge the most "special" someone in my life. For this I would refer you to the post-script of this book at www.hammettco.com.

Appendix: Are You an Asshole?

We all have moments when we behave like an asshole. We get frustrated, angry or perhaps simply exhausted and our darker angels prevail. Usually, when we come to our senses we feel terrible about the way we acted. And hopefully we apologize to those who had to contend with our crass behavior. Yet as we read in this book, there is a difference between occasionally acting like an asshole and engaging in a consistent pattern of bad behavior: behavior that is self-centered, spiteful, vindictive.

The intent of this appendix is to put up a mirror that will allow you to closely reflect on how you behave and ask yourself two straightforward questions:

(1) Am I an asshole? If so, and if this bothers me, I can then address the second question:

(2) Can I change?

SELF-ASSESSMENT

If you've ever thought that maybe, just maybe you're an asshole, then please read through this appendix carefully. Consider the examples, illustrations, and definitions of asshole behavior to be a virtual mirror of sorts. Allow the *reflections* here to give you pause and help you take stock of how you interact with the people in your life.

Leaders at Levels 1 to 5 Compared to Assholes at Levels 1 to 5

In 2001 Jim Collins wrote *Good to Great,* a remarkable book outlining a multiyear research project to address the question: "Can a good company become a great company, and if so, how?" In it, Collins and his researchers framed a hierarchy of leadership that ranges from level 1 (highly capable individual contributor) to level 5 (executive leaders who are marked by humility).

As I considered the research on the destructive behavior of Dark Triad traits it became clear that the behavior of leaders can also be placed on a continuum ranging from ineffective/incompetent to unethical/evil. From this emerged a counter-balance to Collins' Good to Great levels of leaders: a framework for the hierarchy of assholes in organizations.

Collins Levels of Leaders	Hammett's Levels of Asshole Leaders
Level 5: Executive Leader Builds enduring greatness through a paradoxical combination of personal humility and professional will. Puts the interests of others ahead of their own.	**Level 5: Flaming Asshole** Exhibits a predictable pattern of callous, manipulative, arrogant and self-absorbed behavior from which a toxic and harmful workplace environment emerges.
Level 4: Effective Leader Catalyzes commitment to and vigorous pursuit of a clear and compelling vision; stimulates the group to high performance standards.	**Level 4: Sophisticated Asshole** Unlike the leader who's committed to a vision of higher group performance, at this level are committed solely to their own interest. To this end, they place a high value on their political and organizational savvy. They know how to read prevailing opinion and are adept at agreeing with everything yet standing for nothing.

Level 3: Competent Manager	Level 3: Throwback Asshole
Organizes people and resources toward the effective and efficient pursuit of predetermined objectives.	While the competent manager builds towards the future, the leader who is a throwback asshole is stuck in the past. These folks typically rose to a leadership level because of personal connections and alliances, and they believe their leadership position gives them the right to be disrespectful to subordinates.
Level 2: Contributing Team Member Contributes to the achievement of group objectives; works effectively with others in a group setting.	**Level 2: Frustrating Asshole** Leaders at this level have no concept of team or esprit de corps. Rather, they refuse to take accountability for their results, often getting others to do their work while they are quick to take credit for others efforts. They have a strong sense of entitlement and are the last in and the first out. Their influence and subsequent disruption to the team is calculable.

Level 1: Highly Capable Individual	Level 1: Annoying Prick
Makes productive contributions through talent, knowledge, skills, and good work habits.	Leaders at this level are the antitheses of a highly capable individuals. They are individuals who are so miserable with the world and their place in it that they make it their goal to create misery for others. They are under performers who blame others for their lackluster results. While their impact is minimal, others often have to pick up their slack.

In Chapter 8 I use the level framework as a guide for dealing with workplace assholes. However, the framework is also helpful as a simple self-assessment tool. Let me suggest you read though both sets of levels again. This time, ask yourself which side of the table and at which level would people place you? Do people see you as a leader or an asshole?

Traits and Reactions to Watch For

Korn Ferry defines traits as "inclinations, attitudes and natural tendencies a person leans towards, including personality traits and intellectual capacity. Examples include assertiveness, risk-taking, confidence, and aptitude for logic and reasoning." Chapter 3 details the traits associated with the Dark Triad of narcissism, Machiavellism, and psychopathy.

Below I outline the *reactions* from those who are exposed to workplace assholes. As you read this, pay close attention to if you observe these reactions from the people you interact with at work.

- **It's quiet, too quiet.** Because assholes will surround themselves with yes people, they seldom receive critical feedback. They also often react poorly when someone offers helpful advice, so they're less likely to receive this kind of insight in the future. So ask yourself this: "When was the last time someone gave me unvarnished criticism?" I'm not referring to when you overheard someone complaining about how you interact with people. What I'm asking is when was the last time someone offered you considered input on an area that they felt you could improve? If you're having trouble remembering when this last occurred, it should give you pause.

- **Count your friends.** There is a big difference between an acquaintance and a friend. An acquaintance will stand with you as long as it's part of social convention or political expedience. A friend will stand with you no matter what. Ask yourself this: If you didn't hold the position you have, who would continue to hang out with you? Even better, who would you consider a friend outside of your work setting? If you have a tough time coming up with a least a handful of friends, then this should give you pause.

- **Lack of self-awareness.** In chapter 4 I discuss the neuroscience behind self-awareness. In a nutshell, a lack of self-awareness occurs because either you're too self-absorbed to see yourself, or too self-centered to care. Here is the real challenge with self-awareness, we all are bad at correctly assessing how we are doing. A good friend of mine teaches at the University of Chicago. One semester before her class took their final exam, she gave her students a two-question pre-test "(1) How well do you understand the material we covered this semester? (2) How well do you believe you'll do on the final exam?" After the exam she compared the pre-test results with the outcome from the exam. Interestingly, students who felt they knew the material well and would likewise do well on the final scored lower than students who were more guarded in assessing their

152

grasp of the material and projecting of their results on the exam. The only reliable method for gaining a valid self-assessment is to ask those who interact with us most often for their honest, direct feedback. If your self-awareness is based solely on how you feel, and not on insights you've gained from others, then this should give you pause.

When Two Assholes Collide

What happens when two assholes collide? Could this situation perfectly define the ancient paradox: "What happens when an unstoppable force meets an immovable object?" Let's phrase our question differently: What happens when an egocentric, mean-spirited person comes in conflict with someone who is belligerent and hateful? Can there be a winner in this confrontation or does the world implode? In reality, when two assholes collide there's not as much drama as you might anticipate. Here's a real-life example.

In the government sector bad actors collide constantly. While there are many, many dedicated civil servants in government, at times there seems to be just as many self-promoting assholes. I was consulting with several government agencies where I met a senior executive who was clearly a level 4 (sophisticated asshole). Without hesitation I can say this person was the most self-serving, political animal I had ever encountered. They were acutely aware of the power of "optics," and every decision this leader made ran through a filter of "How will this make me look?" Even still, the executive was masterful in navigating the political landscape of the various government agencies with whom she interfaced.

One day, a new administrator was named in an interfacing government agency. Within a few weeks of taking office, it was clear that the person I was coaching had met their match in the new administrator, who themselves was also a level 4 asshole.

Because of my consulting position, I had a unique vantage point to observe these combatants spar. It was like watching a world-class chess match, with both players maneuvering, looking to outwit their opponent. In the end, however, the flaw in the "immovable object" paradox came to light. You see no matter how big of an asshole you are, there is always someone who is bigger. In this case, the new administrator had the upper hand, if for no other reason than they out-ranked the person I was coaching.

What I found amazing was how accurately the person I was coaching was able to call out the selfish and mean-spirited behavior of the new administrator. I recall one occasion sitting in disbelief while the senior executive berated the new administrator, aptly noting their narcissistic actions and highlighting their vindictiveness towards any perceived opponents. Yet the former was totally blind to the fact that all the character traits they saw in the new administrator were traits they themselves exhibited. It reminded me of the saying, "We are more critical of the sins we see in others than the sins we ourselves live each day."

CAN YOU CHANGE

Most requests I receive for leadership coaching come because of a perceived problem in a leader's performance. Perhaps the person is having trouble building a team; or there are concerns with how they are interacting with peers.[54] Whatever the reason for the request, the end goal is the same: "Can you help get 'so-and-so' back on track?" Another way to ask this question would be: "Can you help this leader make the needed changes to improve their leadership effectiveness?" As it relates to this book, the core question is this: "Can an asshat change their behavior?"

When I take on a coaching engagement, I make sure the organization and the leader understand three key questions in the coaching process that center on changing behavior: (1) Do you know, and do you care? (2) Are you able to change, and is there enough time? (3) Is there grace enough to acknowledge change?

---

[54] Herein is a fundamental misperception about leadership coaching: that it is only to be used when a leader is underperforming. Leadership coaching should be leveraged as a resource to build and maintain any leader's effectiveness.

Let me go through these steps individually.

Do you know and Do you care

The best way to describe this step is to share two real-life stories. I mentioned earlier I worked for the CCL, one of the most prestigious organizations in the world dedicated to the science and practice of leadership development. Each year tens of thousands of leaders worldwide attend its development programs. Leaders from nearly every industry, sector, and level take a week out of their lives to attend these programs, which are conducted all over the world. Over time, stories emerged from among the faculty and coaches regarding the leaders who attended these programs. Two stories had a profound impact on me.

The Leader who knew but didn't care—and didn't change

When a leader attends a week-long development program they undergo a significant analysis of their leadership style. Clinical psychologists/leadership coaches review a number of psychometric assessments, 360-degree feedback reports, and insights from interviews with the leader's boss, peers, and director reports. Additionally, they take part in a number of experiential exercises designed to put a spotlight on the participant's leadership style.

During one development program, a well-known executive from a prominent global organization was in attendance. On the next-to-the-last day of the program they had the opportunity to visit with a leadership coach who had reviewed their assessments and observed how the leader engaged in the program exercises. The leadership coach took great care to highlight areas where the executive's approach to leading was creating a toxic work environment in their organization. The coach likewise pointed out how the leader's problematic leadership style was visible by all those participating in the program. The executive was clearly frustrated by the critique and abruptly interrupted the coach:

"Listen, just cut to the chase. Enough with the psychobabble. What's the bottom line?" Without missing a beat, the coach closed the assessments, looked directly at the executive and replied, "It is my clinical assessment that you are an asshole."

The executive paused for a moment then laughingly replied, "No shit. Tell me something I don't know. Let me tell you something. Because of my so-called *poor* leadership style, I make more money than everyone in this building combined. Yeah, I'm an asshole. I've had four wives and they all told me the same thing: I'm an asshole. You know what? I'm just fine with that." There was moment of awkward silence then the coach said, "Well, I guess we're done." The execute left the leadership development program a day early, failing to gain even the slightest benefit from the feedback and coaching.

The Leader who didn't know, yet cared deeply—and changed

In a different program, nearly half a globe away, another leader received very similar feedback. Yet as the leadership coach reviewed the feedback results the executive was deeply bothered. Humbled by the negative impact his leadership style was having on those in his life, he professed a deep desire to make a change in how he interacted with people. A few months after the program, the executive sent a package to the faculty of his leadership program. In it was a handwritten letter and an envelope which had been torn in two.

Here's what was in the handwritten letter:

My Dear Friends,

You will no doubt remember me from the leadership program I attended recently. During the program you gave me the gift of a lifetime. You put a mirror in front of me and gave me a clear look at the kind of person I had become. The image I saw was an ugly, selfish, and hateful asshole. And the damage I had caused in the relationships in my life broke my heart. No more so than that of my wife. To fully understand this let me give you a glimpse into our lives.

As you know I travel a great deal for work. Often when I travel I have my wife drive me to the airport. And on the drive, I write down a list of things I want her to address while I'm away. Occasionally I'll call home while I'm away, and when I do, my attention is on the "list." Seldom do I ask my wife how she's doing. When I return home, my wife picks me up from the airport, and while she drives me home, I go over the list with her. While I do love my wife dearly, my actions rarely showed it. It's the same for those I work with. I care for my staff and all my employees, but I'm so focused on getting things done, achieving the next big milestone, I rarely show my people how much I care for them.

When I returned home from the leadership program, my dear wife was at the airport to get me. This time when she pulled up to get me, I walked over to the driver side of the car and asked her to let me drive. On the way home, I shared with my wife that I'd come to see just how inattentive and self-absorbed I'd been, at home and at work. And that beginning with that very moment I was committing myself to becoming a better husband, a better leader, a better father, and a better man.

My wife sat in silence for what seemed to be an eternity, then she reached into the glovebox and pulled out a legal-sized envelope. She slowly tore the envelope in two and gave it to me. Since I was driving and couldn't really read the envelope, I asked her, "What is this?" She looked at me with tears in her eyes and said quietly, "The divorce papers I asked our lawyer to draw up." We both cried all the way home.

I've got a bit of a journey ahead, but I'm moving in the right direction with my wife, my family, my company, and my people.

Enclosed are the divorce papers my wife tore up and gave me. If you ever have a hard time getting through to an asshole like me, show these papers to them. Hopefully it will be the wake-up call they need.

Are You Able to Change and Is There Enough Time

When I'm coaching a leader who is struggling with leading effectively, the question we need to get to is: "Can the needed changes be made within the given timeframe?"

A while back I was asked by a board of directors to coach a newly hired executive who was creating chaos in an organization by his toxic leadership style. After a few weeks I informed the board I didn't believe the executive would be able to adjust his approach to leading to better fit the organization's culture. My view was that his behavior was based on a lifetime of experiences that reinforced his belief that he was doing the right things the right way.

In the executive's mind he got the position precisely because of the way he led. He was very aware of how his leadership style was affecting employees, and he did care about the success of the organization; yet he did not believe he needed to change. More to the point, he simply did not want to make the effort to adjust his approach to leading, and why would he? By all accounts this guy was successful. His career was marked by ever-increasing levels of responsibility and corresponding salary. In his new role, however, his leadership style simply wasn't working.

Sadly, too often leadership coaching is the last resort in an organization's effort to address a leader's underperformance, with the result that by the time a coach is brought in there isn't time enough to make changes before critical business initiatives fail. A colleague shared with me an occasion when they were brought in to coach a leader who was responsible for the conversion of several billion in assets from one bank to another. Unfortunately, their poor leadership was putting the entire project at risk. The time frame for this conversion was fixed; with significant financial penalties in missing critical deliverables. The reality of the situation was that the organization could not afford the time for the leader to make the needed changes.

Is There Grace Enough to Acknowledge Change

There are also occasions when a leader sees the need to change, is sincere in their desire to change, but too many bridges have been burned. Despite the best efforts of the leader to make the needed changes, the organization will always remember who the leader was and not see the leader for who they've become. Organizational memories can be a hateful thing, especially for people with long tenures.

Adapting Versus Changing

There is a difference between adapting and changing. Adapting is simply putting on a facade: pretending to be something you're not. Change, real change, requires a significant impact to how you think, and this, in turn, impacts how you behave.

Mark Goulston shares a compelling story about when he was faced with a coaching engagement with a senior leader who was a level 5 asshole. After confronting the hard truth that he was indeed acting very badly, the leader asked Goulston a straightforward question: "Is this curable?" His response was sobering: 'Behaving like an asshole is an addiction. It's treatable, but you have to stay with your treatments every day. Otherwise you will slip back into the pull of the Dark Triad.'

As you've read this appendix and possibly felt a sense of conviction regarding how you lead, my last request is that you reflect intently on the following story:

HOW CHANGE SAVED A LIFE

A number of years ago I had the remarkable honor of hearing General Doizier share his story of being rescued from the Red Brigade by Italian Special Forces. In the generals word, here is what happened:

> I had recently been promoted to chief of staff of NATO's Southern European land forces at Verona, Italy. Each morning a driver would come to the apartment where my wife and I lived and take me to the office. On the morning of December 17, 1981,

159

there was a knock at the door. Naturally I assumed it was my driver, and without even a thought, I opened the door. Suddenly several men in ski masks bolted into the apartment and began wrestling me to the ground. I reacted the way any solider would: I fought back, which turned out to be a losing proposition for me and I got beat up pretty good. The last thing I remember seeing before a bag was placed over my head was my wife on the kitchen floor with a gun to her head.

The next thing I recall was waking up inside a tent. After a bit I realized that I was actually inside a tent that was inside a room. I later came to realize I was in a tent that was in the bedroom of a small apartment. Well I knew right off I was in big trouble. My military training taught me that if you are kidnapped and your captors isolate you physically, like I was, it's because they don't want to get too friendly. That way it would be easier to kill you when the time comes.

I knew right off what I had to do; I had to make these guys like me. My life would depend on endearing myself to my captors. If things turned sour and they were going to kill me, I wanted to make this a very hard decision for them. So, I began to do everything opposite of what a brigadier general would do. I didn't command the room. I didn't buck up, act larger than life, impose my will. Every time I was let out of my tent to stretch my legs, I spoke softly and respectfully. And I tried to get to know my captors on a personal level. I asked about their family. I told them about my family. I wanted to—needed to—relate with them.

To be completely truthful, the idea of relating to my captors wasn't an "in the heat of the moment" notion. Just before my promotion to NATO I had the opportunity to participate in a leadership development program where I got direct feedback from coworkers about how I came across. For me the feedback was simple and straightforward. I was a bona fide asshole. And everyone thought so, even my personal friends and family. This was a wake-up call for me. And I made a promise to myself then and there I was going to lead and live differently.

So, on that fateful day in December, I had already been working on coming across differently. Had I not been mindful that I needed to interact with people in a different way, well I'm certain my captors would have gladly shot me just because I was a royal asshole.

After a good laugh we asked the general to finish his story and tell us about the rescue.

I was sitting in my tent, and I could hear arguing outside the bedroom. Then the door burst opened and I could hear what seemed to be several men arguing and shouting. Then there seemed to be a fight. I could hear punches being landed and people falling to the ground. I was certain the argument was about whether to kill me.

After a few moments the fighting stopped and someone unzipped my tent. Then the largest arm I've ever seen in my life reached in and frantically began grabbing for me. I instinctively began pushing and kicking at the arm, knowing this was it. They were going to kill me.

Suddenly a knife cut the tent from end to end. As the tent fell open a heavily armed man in camo grabbed me with one arm and tossed me over his shoulder. I was kicking and fighting for all I was worth. Then in a thick Italian accent this guy yells at me: "General, be still. I'm here to rescue you." He hoisted me up on his shoulder, pulled his side arm, and shot his way out of the room. It was just like what you see in the movies!

General Doizier was convinced that his awareness for interacting with others in a positive way saved his life.

BUILDING A RESUME OR BUILDING A LEGACY

I'm drawn to a thought David Brooks offers in his book *The Road to Character:* There are two sets of virtues, the résumé virtues and the legacy virtues. The résumé virtues are the skills you bring to the marketplace. The legacy virtues are the ones that are talked about when you're not in the room! Deep down we know the legacy virtues are more important than the résumé ones. But our culture spends more time teaching the skills and strategies you need for career success.

Perhaps one question we all should consider is: "What do people say about me when I'm not in the room?" Of course, some will say they don't give a fig what people think of them. All that matters are what they are able to accomplish. This view is rubbish. Unless you have a severe personality disorder, you do care what people think.

Source Notes

Although this book is essentially a practical work, drawing primarily on my professional work, it is informed by a number of scholarly and business sources. Below I list the key resources that provided helpful insights.

Chapter 1: First Things First
Nunberg, G. (2012). *Ascent of the A-word: Assholism, the first sixty years.* New York, NY: Public Affairs.
James, A. (2012). *Assholes: A theory.* New York, NY: Random House.

Chapter 2: The Science of Asshole Behavior
Zimbardo, P. (2007). *The Lucifer effect: Understanding how good people turn evil.* New York, NY: Random House.

Chapter 3: Why People Behave like Assholes—A Psychological View
Furnham, A., Richards, S. C., & Paulhus, D. L. (2013). The Dark Triad of personality: A 10 year review. *Social and Personality Psychology Compass, 7,* 199–216. http://dx.doi.org/10.1111/spc3.12018
American Psychiatric Association. (2013). *Diagnostic and statistical manual of mental disorders* (5th ed.). Author: Washington, D.C.
Spain, S. M., Harms, P. D., & LeBreton, J. M. (2014). The dark side of personality at work. *Journal of Organizational Behavior, 35,* S41–S60. http://doi.org/10.1002/job.1894
Paulhus, D. L., & Williams, K. M. (2002). The Dark Triad of personality: Narcissism, Machiavellianism, and psychopathy. *Journal of Research in Personality, 36,* 556–563. https://doi.org/10.1016/S0092-6566(02)00505-6

Chapter 4: The Neuroscience of Why People Behave like Assholes
Bergland, C. (2013, October). The neuroscience of empathy. *Psychology Today.* https://www.psychologytoday.com/us/blog/the-athletes-way/201310/the-neuroscience-empathy
Silani, G. Lamm, C., Ruff, C. C., & Singer, T. (2013). Right supramarginal gyrus is crucial to overcome emotional egocentricity bias in social judgments. *JNeurosci: The Journal of*

Neuroscience, 33, 15466–15476. https://doi.org/10.1523/
JNEUROSCI.1488-13.2013

Decety, J., Chen, C., Harenski, C., & Kiehl, K. A. (2013). An fMRI
study of affective perspective taking in individuals with
psychopathy: Imagining another in pain does not evoke
empathy. *Frontiers in Human Neuroscience, 7*, 489–500. https://
doi.org/10.3389/fnhum.2013.00489

Dikker, S., & Wan, L., Davidesco, I., Kaggen, L., Oostrik, M.,
McClintock, J., Rowland, J., Michalareas, G., Van Bavel, J. J.,
Ding, M., & Poeppel, D. (2017). Brain-to-brain synchrony
tracks real-world dynamic group interactions in the
classroom. *Current Biology, 27*, 1375–1380. https://
www.cell.com/current-biology/fulltext/
S0960-9822(17)30411-6?_returnURL=https%3A%2F
%2Flinkinghub.elsevier.com%2Fretrieve%2Fpii
%2FS0960982217304116%3Fshowall%3Dtrue

Eisenberger, N. I., & Cole S. W. (2012). Social neuroscience and
health: Neurophysiological mechanisms linking social ties
with physical health. *Nature Neuroscience, 15*(5), 669–674.
https://www.nature.com/articles/nn.3086

Rock, D. (2009). *Your brain at work*. New York, NY. HarperCollins.

Lou, H. C., Changeux, J.-P., & Rosenstand, A. (2017). Towards a
cognitive neuroscience of self-awareness. *Neuroscience &
Biobehavioral Reviews, 83*, 765–773. https://
www.sciencedirect.com/science/article/pii/
S0149763416300410

Ham, T. E., Bonnelle, V., Hellyer, P., Jilka, S., Robertson, I. H., Leech,
R., & Sharp, D. J. (2014). The neural basis of impaired self-
awareness after traumatic brain injury. *Brain, 137*(pt. 2), 586–
597. https://academic.oup.com/brain/article/
137/2/586/284363

Chapter 5: Attraction, Cultural Influences, and Organizational Impact

NPR Marketplace broadcast aired November 9, 2015. "Why so many
bosses are jerks." http://www.marketplace.org/2015/11/09/
life/why-so-many-bosses-are-jerks

Padilla, A., Hogan, R., & Kaiser, R. B. (2007). The toxic triangle:
Destructive leaders, susceptible followers, and conducive
environments. *The Leadership Quarterly, 18*(3), *176–194*.
https://psycnet.apa.org/record/2007-07725-004

Chapter 6: Assholes in the Workplace

http://www.washingtonpost.com/national/health-science/is-your-boss-making-you-sick/2014/10/20/60cd5d44-2953-11e4-8593-da634b334390_story.html
http://www.forbes.com/sites/amyanderson/2014/10/28/a-bad-boss-can-make-you-sick-literally/ http://usatoday30.usatoday.com/news/health/story/2012-08-05/apa-mean-bosses/56813062/1
http://fortune.com/2015/07/16/toxic-coworkers/
http://www.fastcompany.com/3034923/how-to-be-a-success-at-everything/how-to-deal-with-toxic-coworkers-and-keep-your-sanity-in-c

Porath, C. (2016, April). Managing yourself: An antidote to incivility. *Harvard Business Review, 94*(4), 108–111. https://hbr.org/2016/04/an-antidote-to-incivility

Brooks, D. (2012). *The social animal: The hidden sources of love, character, and achievement.* New York, NY: Random House.

Aasland, M. S., Skogstad, A., Notelaers, G., Nielsen, M. B. & Einarsen, S. (2010). The prevalence of destructive leadership behaviour. *British Journal of Management, 21*(2), 438–452. https://www.researchgate.net/publication/227657783_The_Prevalence_of_Destructive_Leadership_Behaviour

Sutton, R. I. (2007). *The no asshole rule: Building a civilized workplace and surviving one that isn't.* New York, NY: Business Plus.

Chamorro-Premuzic, T. (2014, December). The underlying psychology of office politics. *Harvard Business Review, 92*(12). https://hbr.org/2014/12/the-underlying-psychology-of-office-politics

Campbell, W. K., & Miller, J. D. (2011). *The handbook of narcissism and narcissistic personality disorder: Theoretical approaches, empirical findings, and treatments.* Hoboken, NJ: Wiley.

http://archives.drugabuse.gov/StressAlert/stressalert.html#Anchor-Stress-13906

https://hbr.org/2009/04/how-toxic-colleagues-corrode-performance

Siegel, D. J. (2010). *Mindsight: The new science of personal transformation.* New York, NY: Random House.

Twenge, J. M., & Campbell, W. K. (2009). *The narcissism epidemic: Living in the age of entitlement.* New York, NY: Atria.

Porath, C., & Pearson, C. (2009, April). How toxic colleagues corrode performance. *Harvard Business Review, 87*(4). https://hbr.org/2009/04/how-toxic-colleagues-corrode-performance

Dawkins, R. (2006). *The selfish gene* (30th anniversary ed.). Oxford, England: Oxford University Press.

McLeod, L. (2019). How to deal with the 5 most negative types of co-workers. *The Muse.* https://www.themuse.com/advice/how-to-deal-with-the-5-most-negative-types-of-coworkers

Chapter 7: Combating the ARSe Virus

Brooks, D. (2015). *The road to character.* New York, NY: Random House.

Goulston, M. (2010). *Just listen: Discover the secret to getting through to absolutely anyone.* New York, NY: AMACON.

Blackmore, S. (1999). *The meme machine.* Oxford, England: Oxford University Press.

NPR All Things Considered broadcast aired January 6, 2014. Army takes on its own toxic leaders. http://www.npr.org/2014/01/06/259422776/army-takes-on-its-own-toxic-leaders

Siegel, D. J. (2010). *Mindsight: The new science of personal transformation.* New York, NY: Random House.

Twenge, J. M., & Campbell, W. K. (2009). *The narcissism epidemic: Living in the age of entitlement.* New York, NY: Atria.

Morse, G. (2004, October). Executive psychopaths. *Harvard Business Review, 82*(10). http://hbr.org/2004/10/executive-psychopaths

Chapter 8: Dealing with Workplace Assholes

Chappelow, C., Ronayne, P., & Adams, B. (2018). *The toxic boss survival guide: Tactics for navigating the wilderness at work.* Greensboro, NC: Center for Creative Leadership.

Sutton, R. I. (2007). *The no asshole rule: Building a civilized workplace and surviving one that isn't.* New York, NY: Business Plus.

Siegel, D. J. (2010). *Mindsight: The new science of personal transformation.* New York, NY: Random House.

Goulston, M. (2010). *Just listen: Discover the secret to getting through to absolutely anyone.* New York, NY: AMACON.

Ting, S., & Scisco, P. (Eds.). (2006). *The CCL handbook of coaching: A guide for the leader coach.* San Francisco, CA: Wiley.

Riddle, D. D., Hoole, E., & Gullette, E. C. D. (Eds.). (2015). *The Center for Creative Leadership handbook of coaching in organizations.* San Francisco, CA: Wiley.

Chapter 10: Recovering from ARSe

In building my understanding on how to recover from ARSe, I drew heavily on Siegel's book *Mindsight*, especially chapter 8: ("Prisoners of the Past: Memory, Trauma, and Recovery") and chapter 9 ("Making Sense of Our Lives").

Here are several references on the Harvard Study of Adult Development:

http://www.adultdevelopmentstudy.org/grantandglueckstudy

https://www.ted.com/talks/
robert_waldinger_what_makes_a_good_life_lessons_from_the_longest_study_on_happiness

https://well.blogs.nytimes.com/2016/03/23/the-secrets-to-a-happy-life-from-a-harvard-study/?_r=0

Made in the USA
Monee, IL
28 November 2021

83328764R00103